THE OEDIPUS COMPLEX TODAY
Clinical Implications

THE OEDIPUS COMPLEX TODAY

Clinical Implications

Ronald Britton
Michael Feldman
and
Edna O'Shaughnessy

with an introduction by
Hanna Segal

edited by
John Steiner

including Melanie Klein's paper
*The Oedipus Complex
in the Light of Early Anxieties*

Karnac Books
London 1989

First published in 1989 by
H. Karnac (Books) Ltd.
58 Gloucester Road
London SW7 4QY

Second Printing 1991, Third Printing 1995, Fourth Printing 1997
Fifth Printing 2000

British Library Cataloguing in Publication Data

The Oedipus complex today; clinical
implications
1. Children. Development. Role of
Oedipus complex
I. Klein, Melanie. II. Britton, Ronald.
III. Feldman, Michael. IV. O'Shaughnessy, Edna.
155.4'18

ISBN No. 0-946-439-55-9

Printed in Great Britain by Polestar AUP Aberdeen Limited

CONTENTS

PREFACE

The Melanie Klein Conference on the Oedipus Complex, which took place in September 1987, was organized jointly by Professor J. Sandler of the Psychoanalysis Unit at University College, London, and Mrs. Ruth Riesenberg-Malcolm on behalf of the Melanie Klein Trust. It was considered so successful and the three papers presented there seemed to reflect so well the current developments in modern Kleinian views of the Oedipus complex that the Trust decided to have the papers published.

To bring these current views into context we decided to reprint with them Melanie Klein's paper 'The Oedipus complex in the light of early anxieties' (1945). In addition, Dr. Hanna Segal has expanded her introduction which links Klein's paper with the modern work presented here. She also indicates the influence of other post-Kleinian writing, especially that of Bion.

The Tavistock Clinic
120 Belsize Lane
London NW3 5BA

John Steiner

Dr. Ronald Britton is a training analyst of the British Psychoanalytical Society. He was born in the North of England and was educated at the Royal Grammar School, Lancaster. He completed his medical studies at University College, London. Before committing himself full time to psychoanalytic practice, his career had included both adult and child psychiatry. During the 1970s he was Chairman of the Department for Children and Parents at the Tavistock Clinic, where his special interests had been in the provision of psychotherapy for severely deprived and abused children and consulting concerning their care in the community.

Dr. Michael Feldman studied psychology at University College, London, and qualified in medicine at University College Hospital. He trained in psychiatry at the Maudsley Hospital, where he continues to work part-time as consultant psychotherapist and chairman of the psychotherapy unit. For the remainder of his time he works in private practice as a psychoanalyst and as a training analyst of the British Psychoanalytical Society.

Mrs. Edna O'Shaughnessy studied philosophy at Witwatersrand and Oxford Universities, after which she trained as a child psychotherapist at the Tavistock Clinic and worked for many years in the Department of Child Development at the Institute of Education, London University. At present she is a training analyst of the British Psychoanalytical Society and works in private practice as a psychoanalyst of children and adults.

Dr. Hanna Segal has at various times been Scientific Secretary, Chairman of the Education Committee, and President of the British Society and Vice President of the International Psychoanalytical Association, as well as Visiting Professor of the Freud Memorial Chair at University College, London. She is the leading exponent of Melanie Klein's work, about which she has written in numerous papers and two books: *An Introduction to the Work of Melanie Klein* (Heinemann, 1964; reprinted Karnac Books, Institute of Psychoanalysis of London, 1988) and *Melanie Klein* in the Modern Master Series (Fontana 1979). She has also developed her ideas in a number of original papers, which are collected in her third book, *The Work of Hanna Segal* (Jason Aronson, 1981; reprinted Karnac Books, Free Association Books, 1986).

INTRODUCTION

Hanna Segal

Ever since Freud discovered the Oedipus complex it has been recognized as the central conflict in the human psyche—the central cluster of conflicting impulses, phantasies, anxieties and defences. It has therefore become the centre of psychoanalytic work. It is still sometimes mistakenly thought that Klein's work became solely concerned with the baby's relation to the breast and that the role of the father and the Oedipus complex lost in importance in her work. In fact, as is certainly well known by those acquainted with the work, one of Klein's earliest discoveries was that of early forms of the superego and of the Oedipus complex before genital primacy. She discovered that there were primitive forms of the Oedipus complex and that pre-genital does not necessarily mean pre-oedipal. She sees the father—the real father as well as the phantasies about father—as being important in the child's life from the beginning. When she started working with children she was surprised to discover that children not much over two years of age showed oedipal phantasies and had intense anxieties

1

associated with them. Oedipal phantasies gave rise to fear of primitive persecutory figures—maternal, paternal, or as a combined figure often at the very centre of phobias—nightmares and night fears. Those phantasy figures exhibited sadistic oral, urethral and anal features, as well as castration threats, due to the projections of infantile sexuality and sadism, and in keeping with the stage of the child's own psychosexual development. She described the figure of combined sexual parents as an important factor in psychotic anxieties. This phantasy figure is partly a denial of the parental intercourse, combining the two into one monstrous figure, and also a projection of the child's hostility to that intercourse, making it into a particularly threatening figure.

Klein considered that the Oedipus complex starts in the first year of life and is fundamentally affected by the child's relation to the breast. It is the frustration at the breast, and crucially the weaning, that makes the infant turn to the father's penis and become aware of the triangular situation. In her early work she considered that phase as the phase of maximum sadism and, considering that it is the frustration at the breast which initiates the oedipal situation, she also thought that the beginnings of the Oedipus complex are under the aegis of hatred more than of desire and love. Throughout her work with children—as described in *The Psychoanalysis of Children* (1932) and various papers on child and adult analysis—she developed and expanded her views on the Oedipus complex. In 1928 she wrote a paper specifically on the subject, 'Early stages of the Oedipus conflict' (Klein, 1928).

By the time she had formulated the concept of the depressive position, her views on the Oedipus complex had altered in certain important respects. She established the interrelation between the Oedipus complex and the depressive position. The relation to the mother as a whole person, which gradually emerges, then carries the implication of a mother who is separate from the infant and not under the infant's control, having a life of her own, which includes principally a relationship with father, with all that it implies, including feelings of exclusion, envy and jealousy.

But, as in the depressive position, there is more integration and a diminution of paranoid anxieties, and by degrees love and concern take the upper hand over the hatred. Gradually Klein came to the conclusion that the beginnings of the Oedipus complex are not associated with the phase of maximum sadism—an idea she came to discard—but, on the contrary, it is linked with diminishing sadism. The awareness of ambivalence in relation to both parents and to their inter-relationship brings in defences, including some regression to splitting and paranoid anxieties as a defence against guilt. But it also brings in reparative impulses aimed not only at the restoration of the breast and mother, but also, and increasingly, at restoring a good parental couple and a good family as a whole.

In her 1945 paper, 'The Oedipus complex in the light of early anxieties', which we reprint here (chapter one), she spells out clearly the change in her views, as well as making clearer where exactly they differ from Freud's. It is her last paper on the subject, although she refers to the Oedipus complex in nearly all her later papers. For example she wrote,

The infant's capacity to enjoy at the same time the relation to both parents which is an important feature in his mental life and conflicts with his desires prompted by jealousy and anxiety to separate them depends on his feelings that they are separate individuals. This more integrated relation to the parents (which is distinct from the compulsive need to keep the parents apart from one another and to prevent their sexual intercourse) implies the greater understanding of their relation to one another and is a pre-condition for the infant's hope that he can bring them together and unite them in a happy way. [Klein, 1952]

The implications and ramifications of the gradual changes that occur in the psychic organization with the onset of the depressive position are enormous. They include the discovery of ambivalence, sense of loss, guilt, a differentiation between internal and external realities, a capacity for symbolization and many others. The depressive position carries with it, not only change in the nature of the object relationships, but an important change in the whole of mental functioning.

The 1945 paper was written before her major paper, 'Notes on some schizoid mechanisms' (Klein, 1946), in which she describes the paranoid–schizoid position. She never worked out fully the implications of her new discoveries for a complete theory of the Oedipus complex. But she did bring in repeatedly the importance of this primitive constellation on the oedipal situation. For instance, in *Envy and Gratitude* (Klein, 1957) she describes the disastrous consequences if envy rather than jealousy plays a predominant role in the Oedipus complex.

The three papers presented here as chapters two, three and four are based on some of the central ideas addumbrated by Klein, such as the link between the depressive position and the Oedipus complex, and in that context the central importance of the eventual acceptance of a genital creative parental couple and the differentiation between both generations and sexes.

Klein has always emphasized that establishing a good relation to the breast and the mother is essential if the child is to tolerate oedipal anxieties and work them through. Since then a great deal of work has been done based on

Klein's central ideas. Her discovery of the role of projective identification in the paranoid–schizoid position has been developed and gave rise to a more detailed understanding of the early pathology, and particularly the role of pathological forms of projective identification. All three authors use Bion's concept of the container and the contained as the prototype for the perceptions and experiences of the relationships between the parents (Bion, 1962, 1963).

Bion extends Klein's concept of projective identification to include a primitive mental communication and interchange. The infant projects into the breast his anxiety and inchoate primitive concrete elements (beta elements). A mother capable of containing projective identification unconsciously processes those projections and responds adequately to the infant's need. When this happens, the infant can reintroject his projections, modified by understanding, and he also introjects the breast as a container capable of containing and dealing with anxiety. This forms the basis of his own capacity to deal with anxiety. This modification by understanding transforms the beta elements into alpha elements—a higher level of mental functioning. According to Bion, a good relationship between container and contained is the basis of such later capacities as symbolizing and thinking. When the relation is severely disturbed by mother's adverse response or the infant's envy—usually a combination of both—it lays the basis for later psychotic disturbance.

The three chapters are concerned with the primitive forms of the Oedipus complex, the combined parental figure, the role of projective identification and primitive psychotic forms of the Oedipus complex, either as a regressive defence or because the pre-oedipal psychotic process makes the emergence of a proper Oedipus situation impossible. A bad relation between container and contained affects crucially the beginning of the Oedipus complex. Bion (1970) suggested that in a good ('commensal') relationship between container and contained, the two objects 'share a third to the advantage of all three'. A bad ('parasitic') relationship, however, 'produces a third which is destructive of all three'.

As I see it, in order to preserve a tolerable relation to the breast, the infant splits off the bad aspects from both the breast and himself and creates a bad third figure. The father's penis is an ideal container for such projections. In all three chapters patients are described whose phantasy life is dominated by such bad figures, the intrusion of which is felt to be catastrophic to the relation between the child and the mother. Splitting mechanisms are also in evidence. In chapter one Melanie Klein describes in Richard how an early splitting of the breast affects his Oedipus complex. He splits between an ideal-breast mother and a bad father and a bad genital mother containing the father. However, those splits and projections are more like a regression to a more normal paranoid–schizoid position than is the case with the more disturbed patients presented by Drs. Britton and Feldman and Mrs. O'Shaughnessy. Mrs. O'Shaughnessy describes a particular kind of splitting, which she calls 'fracturing' the parental couple, which attacks its heterosexual procreative qualities. The couple is broken apart, or fractured, into two sexual halves: one a sadistic phallus, the other a weakened masochistic female, both in phantasy felt to be ready for homosexual alliances against the other. This splitting is different in kind and imbued with far greater violence than the material of Mrs. Klein's Richard.

All three authors, but in particular Dr. Feldman, illustrate the way the patient's phantasy concerning the nature of the parental relationship not only affects the quality of his object relations and the nature of his anxieties and defences but has a profound effect on his thinking. Dr. Feldman shows how the way the parental couple come together in these phantasies, especially whether this is lively and pleasurable or destructive, will determine the way he experiences his own thoughts coming together in his mind. Thinking necessitates making links including the links between the parents which is what patients with disturbances in the early oedipal situation cannot bear. This is further illustrated by Dr. Britton's patient who experiences her analyst's thinking as parental intercourse and shouts, 'Stop that fucking thinking'.

From the beginning of her work with children Melanie Klein was concerned with the epistimophilic drives. She connected those with the urge to explore the maternal body, and she connected the inhibitions in learning with paranoid anxieties about the maternal body. The authors of the three chapters presented here emphasize the link between the epistomophilic drives and the discovery of the parental intercourse.

Dr. Britton formulates in an interesting way the oedipal triangle in the depressive position as defining a particular mental space within the boundary of the triangle. In this mental space the child can maintain differentiated relations with each parent, contrasting with the primitive relation to a combined parental figure, whilst recognizing at the same time the existence of the parents as a couple, with himself as an outsider—the existence of such a mental space affecting fundamentally a freedom of mental processes. This mental space, according to Dr. Britton, is an extension of the original relation between the container and the contained as described by Bion. Certainly the original relation between the container and the contained is the basis of a later concept of the relationship between the penis and the vagina. However, there is an important difference. In the original situation the child is a participant and a beneficiary of that relationship. Recognizing the parental couple confronts him with a good contained–container relationship from which he is excluded. It confronts him with separateness and separation as part of the working through of the depressive position. It also confronts him with the recognition that the nature of the link between the parents is different in kind from the relation of the child to the parents and at the moment unavailable to him. This is an interesting extension of Bion's concept. It is also a new angle on the momentous changes in the mental functioning that occur in the depressive position.

I would like to add a point to the idea as described by Dr. Britton. An important part of the difference between the infant's relation to the parents and their relationship is not only that they exchange genital gratifications, but also—and, I think, importantly—the fact that the parental intercourse leads to the creation of a new baby. This is always so in phantasy, even if in reality there is no new sibling. When I think of Dr. Britton's triangle as defining the space in which different links can be established between the child and the two parents, I think that space implicitly contains the room for a new baby. If a new baby appears inside mother, as in the case of Mrs. O'Shaughnessy's child patient, before such a space can be established—and while the little infant is still heavily dependent on the phantasy of getting back inside mother—psychotic disturbances can easily ensue.

All the chapters are based on central concepts first put forward by Mrs. Klein. They show, however, a considerable development and elaboration of her basic ideas. For instance, though Mrs. Klein established the existence of primitive and psychotic forms of the Oedipus complex, the chapters presented show how much work has been done in studying those early phenomena clinically. They also show a considerable advance in understanding the effect of those early processes and phantasies on such mental functions as perception and thinking. All of the chapters have to do with the distortions of thinking.

All the chapters are also concerned with technique, and it is in this area that developments since Mrs. Klein are possibly most striking. They are concerned with the effect of primitive acting in the psychoanalytic session. They describe the constant pressure on the analyst to play a role in the primitive oedipal drama and the potentially disruptive effects on the analyst's own thinking. In psychoanalysis, theory and technique are closely interrelated. It is the clinical and technical challenge that leads the psychoanalyst to modify and refine his theoretical framework, and this is the way psychoanalytic theory grows. I think the chapters presented here are evidence of the continuing vitality and development of Freud's and Klein's ideas.

REFERENCES

Bion, W. R. (1962). *Learning from Experience*. London: Heinemann. [Reprinted London: Karnac Books, Maresfield Library, 1984.]

———— (1963). *Elements of Psycho-analysis*. London: Heinemann. [Reprinted London: Karnac Books, Maresfield Library, 1984.]

———— (1970). *Attention and Interpretation*. London: Tavistock. [Reprinted London: Karnac Books, Maresfield Library, 1984.]

Klein, M. (1928). Early stages of the Oedipus conflict. *Int. J. Psycho-Anal.*, *9*, 167–180. [Reprinted in *The Writings of Melanie Klein, 1* (pp. 186–198). London: Hogarth Press, 1975.]

———— (1932). *The Psychoanalysis of Children*. [Reprinted in *The Writings of Melanie Klein, 2*. London: Hogarth Press, 1975.]

———— (1935). A contribution to the psychogenesis of manic-depressive states. *Int. J. Psycho-Anal.*, *16*, 145–174. [Reprinted in *The Writings of Melanie Klein, 1* (pp. 262–289). London: Hogarth Press, 1975.]

———— (1946). Notes on some schizoid mechanisms. *Int. J. Psycho-Anal.*, *27*, 99–110. [Reprinted in *The Writings of Melanie Klein, 3* (pp. 1–24). London: Hogarth Press, 1975.]

———— (1952). Some theoretical conclusions regarding the emotional life of the infant. In *Developments in Psychoanalysis,* with Heimann, Isaacs & Riviere. [Reprinted in *The Writings of Melanie Klein, 3* (pp. 61–93). London: Hogarth Press, 1975.]

———— (1957). *Envy and Gratitude.* London: Tavistock. [Reprinted in *The Writings of Melanie Klein, 3* (pp. 176–235). London: Hogarth Press, 1975.]

CHAPTER ONE

The Oedipus complex in the light of early anxieties (1945)

Melanie Klein

INTRODUCTION

I have two main objectives in presenting this paper. I intend to single out some typical early anxiety situations and show their connection with the Oedipus complex. Since these anxieties and defences are part of the infantile depressive position as I see it, I hope to throw some light on the relation between the depressive position and libidinal development. My second purpose is to compare my conclusions about the Oedipus complex with Freud's views on that subject.

Reprinted from Melanie Klein, *Love, Guilt and Reparation,* copyright © 1983 by The Hogarth Press; by permission of the estate of the author and The Hogarth Press. First published in *Int. J. Psycho-Anal.* *26* (1945): 11–33.

Useful explanatory notes to this paper have been written by Edna O'Shaughnessy (1975).

11

I shall exemplify my argument by short extracts from two case histories. Many more details could be adduced about both analyses about the patients' family relationships and about the technique used. I shall, however, confine myself to those details of the material which are most essential from the point of view of my subject-matter.

The children whose case histories I shall use to illustrate my argument were both suffering from severe emotional difficulties. In making use of such material as a basis for my conclusions about the normal course of the Oedipus development, I am following a method well tried in psycho-analysis. Freud justified this angle of approach in many of his writings. For instance in one place, he says: 'Pathology has always done us the service of making discernible by isolation and exaggeration conditions which would remain concealed in a normal state.' (*S.E.* **22**, p. 121).

EXTRACTS FROM CASE HISTORY ILLUSTRATING THE BOY'S OEDIPUS DEVELOPMENT

The material on which I shall draw to illustrate my views about the boy's Oedipus development is taken from the analysis of a boy of ten. His parents felt impelled to seek help for him since some of his symptoms had developed to such an extent that it became impossible for him to attend school. He was very much afraid of children and because of this fear he more and more avoided going out by himself. Moreover, for some years a progressive inhibition of his faculties and interests caused great concern to his parents. In addition to these symptoms, which prevented him from attending school, he was excessively preoccupied with his health and was frequently subject to depressed moods. These difficulties showed themselves in his appearance, for he looked very worried and unhappy. At times, however—

and this became striking during analytic sessions—his depression lifted and then sudden life and sparkle came into his eyes and transformed his face completely.

Richard was in many ways a precocious and gifted child. He was very musical and showed this already at an early age. He had a pronounced love of nature, but only of nature in its pleasant aspects. His artistic gifts showed, for instance, in the ways in which he chose his words and in a feeling for the dramatic which enlivened his conversation. He could not get on with children and was at his best in adult company, particularly in the company of women. He tried to impress them by his conversational gifts and to ingratiate himself with them in a rather precocious way.

Richard's suckling period had been short and unsatisfactory. He had been a delicate infant and had suffered from colds and illnesses from infancy onwards. He had undergone two operations (circumcision and tonsillectomy) between his third and sixth year. The family lived in modest but not uncomfortable circumstances. The atmosphere in the home was not altogether happy. There was a certain lack of warmth and of common interests between his parents, though no open trouble. Richard was the second of two children, his brother being a few years his senior. His mother, though not ill in a clinical sense, was a depressive type. She was very worried about any illness in Richard, and there was no doubt that her attitude had contributed to his hypochondriacal fears. Her relation to Richard was in some ways not satisfactory; while his elder brother was a great success at school and absorbed most of the mother's capacity for love, Richard was rather a disappointment to her. Though he was devoted to her, he was an extremely difficult child to deal with. He had no interests and hobbies to occupy him. He was over-anxious and over-affectionate towards his mother and clung to her in a persistent and exhausting way.

His mother lavished much care on him and in some ways pampered him, but she had no real appreciation of the less obvious sides of his character, such as a great inherent capacity for love and kindness. She failed to understand that the child loved her very much, and she had little confidence in his future development. At the same time she was on the whole patient in dealing with him; for instance she did not attempt to press the company of other children on him or to force him to attend school.

Richard's father was fond of him and very kind to him, but he seemed to leave the responsibility for the boy's upbringing predominantly to his mother. As the analysis showed, Richard felt that his father was too forbearing with him and exerted his authority in the family circle too little. His elder brother was on the whole friendly and patient with Richard, but the two boys had little in common.

The outbreak of the war had greatly increased Richard's difficulties. He was evacuated with his mother, and moved with her for the purpose of his analysis to the small town where I was staying at the time, while his brother was sent away with his school. Parting from his home upset Richard a good deal. Moreover the war stirred all his anxieties, and he was particularly frightened of air-raids and bombs. He followed the news closely and took a great interest in the changes in the war situation, and this preoccupation came up again and again during the course of the analysis.

Though there were difficulties in the family situation—as well as serious difficulties in Richard's early history—in my view the severity of his illness could not be explained by those circumstances alone. As in every case, we have to take into consideration the internal processes resulting from, and interacting with, constitutional as well as environmental factors; but I am unable to deal here in detail with the interaction of all these factors. I shall restrict myself to showing the influence of certain early anxieties on genital development.

The analysis took place in a small town some distance from London, in a house whose owners were away at the time. It was not the kind of playroom I should have chosen, since I was unable to remove a number of books, pictures, maps, etc. Richard had a particular, almost personal relation to this room and to the house, which he identified with me. For instance, he often spoke affectionately about it and to it, said good-bye to it before leaving at the end of an hour, and sometimes took great care in arranging the furniture in a way which he felt would make the room 'happy'.

In the course of the analysis Richard produced a series of drawings.[1] One of the first things he drew was a starfish hovering near a plant under water, and he explained to me that it was a hungry baby which wanted to eat the plant. An octopus, much bigger than the starfish and with a human face, entered into his drawings a day or two later. This octopus represented his father and his father's genital in their dangerous aspects and was later unconsciously equated with the 'monster' which we shall presently encounter in the material. The starfish shape soon led to a pattern drawing made up of different coloured sections. The four main colours in this type of drawing—black, blue, purple and red—symbolized his father, mother, brother and himself respectively. In one of the first drawings in which these four colours were used he introduced black and red by marching the pencils towards the drawing with accompanying noises. He explained that black was his father, and accompanied the movement of the pencil by imitating the

[1]The accompanying reproductions are traced from the originals and somewhat reduced in size. The originals were drawn in pencil and coloured with crayons. The different colours have as far as possible been indicated by different markings. In *Drawing III,* however, the submarines should be black, the flags red, and the fishes and starfish yellow.

sound of marching soldiers. Red came next, and Richard said it was himself and sang a cheerful tune as he moved up the pencil. When colouring the blue sections he said this was his mother, and when filling in the purple sections he said his brother was nice and was helping him.

The pattern represented an empire, the different sections standing for different countries. It is significant that his interest in the events of the war played an important part in his associations. He often looked up on the map the countries which Hitler had subjugated, and the connection between the countries on the map and his own empire drawings was evident. The empire drawings represented his mother, who was being invaded and attacked. His father usually appeared as the enemy; Richard and his brother figured in the drawings in various rôles, sometimes as allies of his mother, sometimes as allies of his father.

These pattern drawings, though superficially similar, varied greatly in detail—in fact we never had two exactly alike. The way he made these drawings, or for that matter most of his drawings, was significant. He did not start out with any deliberate plan and was often surprised to see the finished picture.

He used various sorts of play material; for instance the pencils and crayons with which he made his drawings also figured in his play as people. In addition he brought his own set of toy ships, two of which always stood for his parents, while the other ships appeared in varying rôles.

For purposes of exposition I have restricted my selection of material to a few instances, mainly drawn from six analytic hours. In these hours—partly owing to external circumstances which I shall discuss later—certain anxieties had temporarily come more strongly to the fore. They were diminished by interpretation, and the resulting changes threw light on the influence of early anxieties on genital development. These changes, which were only a step towards fuller genitality and stability, had already been foreshadowed earlier on in Richard's analysis.

With regard to the interpretations adduced in this paper, it goes without saying that I have selected those which were most relevant to my subject matter. I shall make clear which interpretations were given by the patient himself. In addition to interpretations which I gave to the patient, the paper contains a number of conclusions drawn from the material, and I shall not at every point make a clear distinction between these two categories. A consistent demarcation of such a kind would involve a good deal of repetition and blur the main issues.

Early anxieties impeding Oedipus development

I take as my starting point the resumption of the analysis after a break of ten days. The analysis had by then lasted six weeks. During this break I was in London, and Richard went away on holiday. He had never been in an air-raid, and his fears of air-raids centred on London as the place most in danger. Hence to him my going to London meant going to destruction and death. This added to the anxiety which was stirred up in him by the interruption of the analysis.

On my return I found Richard very worried and depressed. During the whole first hour he hardly looked at me, and alternated between sitting rigidly on his chair without lifting his eyes and wandering out restlessly into the adjoining kitchen and into the garden. In spite of his marked resistance he did, however, put a few questions to me: Had I seen much of 'battered' London? Had there been an air-raid while I was there? Had there been a thunderstorm in London?

One of the first things he told me was that he hated returning to the town where the analysis took place, and called the town a 'pig-sty' and a 'nightmare'. He soon went out into the garden, where he seemed more free to look around. He caught sight of some toadstools which he showed to me, shuddering and saying they were poisonous. Back in the room, he picked up a book from the shelf and particularly pointed out to me a picture of a little man fighting against an 'awful monster'.

On the second day after my return Richard told me with great resistance about a conversation he had had with his mother while I was away. He had told his mother that he was very worried about his having babies later on and had asked her whether it would hurt very much. In reply she had, not for the first time, explained the part played by the man in reproduction, whereupon he had said he would not like to put his genital into somebody else's genital: that would frighten him, and the whole thing was a great worry to him.

In my interpretation I linked this fear with the 'pig-sty' town; it stood in his mind for my 'inside' and his mother's 'inside', which had turned bad because of thunderstorms and Hitler's bombs. These represented his 'bad' father's penis entering his mother's body and turning it into an endangered and dangerous place. The 'bad' penis inside his mother was also symbolized by the poisonous toadstools which had grown in the garden in my absence, as well as by the monster against which the little man (representing himself) was fighting. The phantasy that his mother contained the destructive genital of his father accounted in part for his fears of sexual intercourse. This anxiety had been stirred up and intensified by my going to London. His own aggressive wishes relating to his parents' sexual intercourse greatly added to his anxieties and feelings of guilt.

There was a close connection between Richard's fear of his 'bad' father's penis inside his mother and his phobia of children. Both these fears were closely bound up with the phantasies about his mother's 'inside' as a place of danger. For he felt he had attacked and injured the imaginary babies inside his mother's body and they had become his enemies. A good deal of this anxiety was transferred on to children in the external world.

The first thing Richard did with his fleet during these hours was to make a destroyer, which he named 'Vampire', bump into the battleship 'Rodney', which always represented his mother. Resistance set in at once and he quickly rearranged the fleet. However, he did reply—though reluctantly—when I asked him who the 'Vampire' stood for, and said it was himself. The sudden resistance, which had made him interrupt his play, threw some light on the repression of his genital desires towards his mother. The bumping of one ship against another had repeatedly in his analysis turned out to symbolize sexual intercourse. One of the main causes of the repression of his genital desires was his fear of the destructiveness of sexual intercourse because—as the name 'Vampire' suggests—he attributed to it an oral-sadistic character.

I shall now interpret *Drawing I,* which further illustrates Richard's anxiety situations at this stage of the analysis. In the pattern drawings, as we already know, red always stood for Richard, black for his father, purple for his brother and light blue for his mother. While colouring the red sections Richard said: 'These are the Russians.' Though the Russians had become our allies, he was very suspicious of them. Therefore, in referring to red (himself) as the suspect Russians, he was showing me that he was afraid of his own aggression. It was this fear which had made him stop the fleet game at the moment when he realized that he was being the 'Vampire' in his sexual approach to his mother.

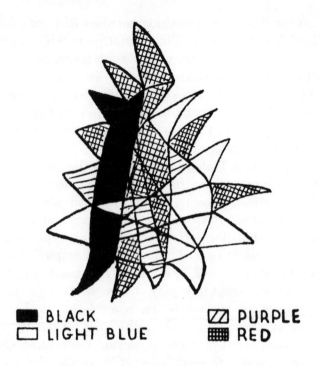

■ BLACK   ▨ PURPLE
☐ LIGHT BLUE   ▦ RED

I

Drawing I expressed his anxieties about his mother's body, attacked by the bad Hitler-father (bombs, thunderstorms, poisonous toadstools). As we shall see when we discuss his associations to *Drawing II,* the whole empire represented his mother's body and was pierced by his own 'bad' genital. In *Drawing I,* however, the piercing was done by three genitals, representing the three men in the family: father, brother and himself. We know that during this hour Richard had expressed his horror of sexual intercourse. To the phantasy of destruction threatening his mother from his 'bad' father was added the danger to her from Richard's aggression, for he identified himself with his 'bad' father. His brother too appeared as an attacker. In this drawing his mother (light blue) contains the bad men, or ultimately their bad genitals, and her body is therefore endangered and a place of danger.

Some early defences

Richard's anxiety about his aggression, and particularly about his oral-sadistic tendencies, was very great and led to a sharp struggle in him against his aggression. This struggle could at times be plainly seen. It is significant that in moments of anger he ground his teeth and moved his jaws as if he were biting. Owing to the strength of his oral-sadistic impulses he felt in great danger of harming his mother. He often asked, even after quite harmless remarks to his mother or to myself: 'Have I hurt your feelings?' The fear and guilt relating to his destructive phantasies moulded his whole emotional life. In order to retain his love for his mother, he again and again attempted to restrain his jealousy and grievances, denying even obvious causes for them.

However, Richard's attempts to restrain his hatred and aggressiveness and to deny his grievances were not successful. The repressed anger about frustrations in the past and present came out clearly in the transference situation—for instance, in his response to the frustration imposed on him by the interruption of the analysis. We know that by going to London I had become in his mind an injured object. I was not, however, injured only through being exposed to the danger of bombs, but also because by frustrating him I had aroused his hatred; in consequence he felt unconsciously that he had attacked me. In repetition of earlier situations of frustration, he had become—in his phantasied attacks on me—identified with the bombing and dangerous Hitler-father, and he feared retaliation. I therefore turned into a hostile and revengeful figure.

The early splitting of the mother figure into a good and

bad 'breast mother' as a way of dealing with ambivalence had been very marked in Richard. This division developed further into a division between the 'breast mother' who was 'good' and the 'genital mother' who was 'bad'. At this stage of the analysis, his actual mother stood for the 'good breast mother', while I had become the 'bad genital mother', and I therefore aroused in him the aggression and fears connected with that figure. I had become the mother who is injured by the father in sexual intercourse, or is united with the 'bad' Hitler-father.

That Richard's genital interests had been active at that time was shown, for instance, by his conversation with his mother about sexual intercourse, though at the time he predominantly expressed horror. But it was this horror which made him turn away from me as the 'genital' mother and drove him to his actual mother as the good object. This he achieved by a regression to the oral stage. While I was in London, Richard was more than ever inseparable from his mother. As he put it to me, he was 'Mum's chick' and 'chicks do run after their Mums'. This flight to the breast mother, as a defence against anxiety about the genital mother, was not successful. For Richard added: 'But then chicks have to do without them, because the hens don't look after them any more and don't care for them.'

The frustration experienced in the transference situation through the interruption of the analysis had revived earlier frustrations and grievances, and fundamentally the earliest deprivation suffered in relation to his mother's breast. Therefore the belief in the good mother could not be maintained.

Immediately after the collision between 'Vampire' (himself) and 'Rodney' (his mother), which I have described in the previous section, Richard put the battleships 'Rodney' and 'Nelson' (his mother and father) side by side, and then, in a row lengthwise, some ships representing his brother, himself and his dog, arranged—as he said—in order of age. Here the fleet game was expressing his wish to restore harmony and peace in the family, by allowing his parents to come together and by giving way to his father's and brother's authority. This implied the need to restrain jealousy and hatred, for only then, he felt, could he avoid the fight with his father for the possession of his mother. In that way he warded off his castration fear and moreover preserved the good father and the good brother. Above all, he also saved his mother from being injured in the fight between his father and himself.

Thus Richard was not only dominated by the need to defend himself against the fear of being attacked by his rivals, his father and brother, but also by concern for his good objects. Feelings of love and the urge to repair damage done in phantasy—damage which would be repeated if he gave way to his hatred and jealousy—came out in greater strength.

Peace and harmony in the family, however, could only be achieved, jealousy and hatred could only be restrained, and the loved objects could only be preserved if Richard repressed his Oedipus wishes. The repression of his Oedipus wishes implied a partial regression to babyhood, but this regression was bound up with the *idealization* of the mother-and-baby relationship. For he wished to turn himself into an infant free from aggression, and in particular free from oral-sadistic impulses. The idealization of the baby presupposed a corresponding idealization of the mother, in the first place of her breasts: an ideal breast which never frustrates, a mother and child in a purely loving relation to each other. The bad breast, the bad mother, was kept widely apart in his mind from the ideal mother.

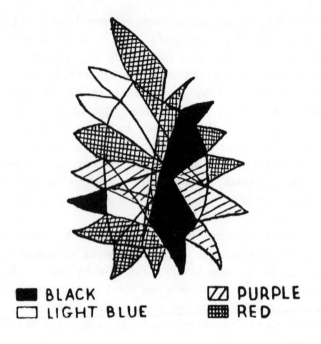

■ BLACK   ▨ PURPLE
□ LIGHT BLUE   ▦ RED

II

Drawing II illustrates some of Richard's methods of dealing with ambivalence, anxiety and guilt. He pointed out to me the red section 'which goes all through Mum's empire', but quickly corrected himself, saying: 'It's not Mum's empire, it's just an empire where all of us have some countries.' I interpreted that he was afraid to realize that he meant it to be his mother's empire because then the red section would be piercing his mother's inside. Thereupon Richard, looking at the drawing once more, suggested that this red section looked 'like a genital', and he pointed out that it divided the empire into two: in the West there were countries belonging to everybody, while the part in the East did not contain anything of his mother—but only himself, his father and his brother.

The left-hand side of the drawing represented the good mother in close association with Richard, for there was little of his father and relatively little of his brother on that side of the drawing. In contrast, on the right side (the 'dangerous East' which I had encountered before in his analysis) only the fighting men or rather their bad genitals appeared. His mother had disappeared from this side of the drawing because, as he felt it, she had been overwhelmed by the bad men. This drawing expressed the division into the endangered bad mother (the genital mother) and the loved and safe mother (the breast mother).

In the first drawing, which I have used to illustrate certain anxiety situations, we can already see something of the defence mechanisms which are more clearly shown in *Drawing II*. Though in *Drawing I* the light-blue mother is spread all over the picture, and the splitting into 'genital' mother and 'breast' mother has not come about as clearly as in *Drawing II,* an attempt at a division of this kind can be seen if we isolate the section on the extreme right.

It is illuminating that in *Drawing II* the division is effected by a particularly sharp and elongated section which Richard interpreted as a genital. In this way he expressed his belief that the male genital was piercing and dangerous. This section looks like a long sharp tooth or like a dagger, and in my view expresses both these meanings: the former symbolizing the danger to the loved object from the oral-sadistic impulses, the latter the danger pertaining, as he felt, to the genital function as such because of its penetrating nature.

These fears contributed again and again to his flight to the 'breast' mother. He could achieve relative stability only on a predominantly pre-genital level. The forward movement of the libido was impeded, because anxiety and guilt were too great and the ego was unable to evolve adequate defences. Thus the genital organization could not be sufficiently stabilized,[1] which implied a strong tendency to regression. The interplay between the phenomena of fixation and regression could be seen at every step of his development.

Diminished repression of Oedipus desires

The analysis of the various anxiety situations which I have described had the effect of bringing Richard's Oedipus desires and anxieties more fully to the fore. But his ego could only maintain those desires by the strengthened use of certain defences (which I shall deal with in this section). These defences, however, could only become effective because some anxiety had been lessened by analysis, and this also implied a lessening of fixations.

When the repression of Richard's genital desires was to some extent lifted, his castration fear came more fully under analysis and found expression in various ways, with a corresponding modification in his methods of defence. In the third hour after my return Richard went out into the garden and spoke of his wish to climb mountains, particularly

---

[1]Freud in his 'Infantile Genital Organization of the Libido', (*S.E.* **19**), described the infantile genital organization as a 'phallic phase'. One of his main reasons for introducing this term was his view that during the infantile genital phase the female genital is not yet discovered or acknowledged, and that the whole interest centres on the penis. My experience does not confirm this point of view; and I do not think that the use of the term 'phallic' would cover the material under discussion in this paper. I am therefore keeping to Freud's original term 'genital phase' (or 'genital organization'). I shall give my reasons for this choice of terms more fully in the general theoretical summary later in this paper.

Snowdon, which he had mentioned earlier in the course of his analysis. While he was talking he noticed clouds in the sky and suggested that a dangerous storm was gathering. On such days, he said, he felt sorry for mountains which have a bad time when a storm breaks over them. This expressed his fear of the bad father, represented by bombs and thunderstorms in the earlier material. The wish to climb Snowdon, symbolizing his desire for sexual intercourse with his mother, at once called up the fear of castration by the bad father, and the storm which was breaking thus meant a danger to his mother as well as to himself.

During the same hour Richard told me that he was going to make five drawings. He mentioned that he had seen a swan with four 'sweet' cygnets. In playing with the fleet, Richard allocated one ship to me and one to himself; I was going on a pleasure trip in my ship and so was he in his. At first he moved his ship away, but soon brought it round and put it quite close to mine. This touching of ships had in former material—particularly in relation to his parents— repeatedly symbolized sexual intercourse. In this play, therefore, Richard was expressing his genital desires as well as his hope for potency. The five drawings he said he was going to give me represented himself (the swan) giving me—or rather his mother—four children (the cygnets).

A few days earlier, as we have seen, there had been a similar incident in the fleet game: 'Vampire' (Richard) touching 'Rodney' (his mother). At that time it had led to an abrupt change of play caused by Richard's fear lest his genital desires should be dominated by his oral-sadistic impulses. During the following few days, however, anxiety was in some measure relieved, aggression was lessened, and concurrently some methods of defence became strengthened. Hence a similar play incident (his ship touching mine on the pleasure trip) could now take place without giving rise to anxiety and to the repression of his genital desires.

Richard's growing belief that he would achieve potency was bound up with a greater hope that his mother could be preserved. He was now able to allow himself the phantasy that she would love him as a man and permit him to take his father's place. This led to the hope that she would become his ally and protect him against all his rivals. For instance, Richard took the blue crayon and the red crayon (his mother and himself) and stood them up side by side on the table. Then the black crayon (his father) was marched towards them and was driven off by the red crayon, while the blue crayon drove off the purple one (his brother). This play expressed Richard's wish that his mother, in unison with himself, should drive off his dangerous father and brother. His mother as a strong figure, fighting against the bad men and their dangerous genitals, also appeared in an association to *Drawing II,* for he said that the blue mother in the West was preparing to fight the East and regain her countries there. As we know, on the right-hand side of *Drawing II* she had been overwhelmed by the genital attacks of the three men, his father, his brother and himself. In *Drawing IV,* which I shall describe a little later, Richard, by extending the blue over most of the drawing, expressed his hope that his mother would regain her lost territory. Then—restored and revived—she would be able to help and protect him. Because of this hope of restoring and reviving his good object, which implied his belief that he could cope more successfully with his aggression, Richard was able to experience his genital desires more strongly. Also, since his anxiety was lessened, he could turn his aggression outwards and take up in phantasy the fight with his father and brother for the possession of his mother. In his play with the fleet he arranged his ships to form one long row, with the smallest ship in front. The meaning of this game

was that he had annexed his father's and brother's genitals and added them to his own. He felt that by this
phantasied victory over his rivals he had achieved
potency.

Drawing III is one of a series of drawings in which plants,
starfishes, ships and fishes figured in various combinations,
and which appeared frequently during the analysis. Just as
in the type of drawing representing the empire, there was a
great variation in details, but certain elements always
presented the same object and situation. The plants
underneath the water stood for his mother's genitals; there
were usually two plants with a space in between. The plants
also stood for his mother's breasts, and when one of the
starfishes was in between the plants, this invariably meant
that the child was in possession of his mother's breasts or
having sexual intercourse with her. The jagged points in the
shape of the starfish represented teeth and symbolized the
baby's oral-sadistic impulses.

In starting *Drawing III* Richard first drew the two ships,
then the large fish and some of the little ones around it.
While drawing these, he became more and more eager and
alive and filled in the space with baby fishes. Then he drew
my attention to one of the baby fishes being covered by a fin
of the 'Mum-fish' and said: 'This is the youngest baby.' The
drawing suggests that the baby fish was being fed by the
mother. I asked Richard whether he was among the little
fishes, but he said he was not. He also told me that the
starfish between the plants was a grown-up person and that
the smaller starfish was a half-grown person, and explained
that this was his brother; he also pointed out that the
'Sunfish' periscope was 'sticking into Rodney'. I suggested to
him that the 'Sunfish' represented himself (the sun
standing for the son) and that the periscope sticking into
'Rodney' (the mother) meant his sexual intercourse with his
mother.

III

Richard's statement that the starfish between the plants was a grown-up person implied that it stood for his father, while Richard was represented by the 'Sunfish', the ship which was even bigger than 'Rodney' (his mother). In this way he expressed the reversal of the father-son relation. At the same time he indicated his love for his father, and his wish to make reparation, by putting the starfish-father between the plants and thus allotting him the position of a gratified child.

The material presented in this section shows that the positive Oedipus situation and genital position had come more fully to the fore. Richard had, as we have seen, achieved this by various methods. One of them was to make his father into the baby—a baby which was not deprived of gratification and therefore would be 'good'—while he himself annexed his father's penis.

Until then Richard, who appeared in various rôles in this type of drawing, had always recognized himself in the rôle of the child as well. For under the stress of anxiety he retreated to the idealized rôle of the gratified and loving infant. Now he stated for the first time that he was not among the babies in the picture. This seemed to me another indication of the strengthening of his genital position. He now felt that he could grow up and become sexually potent. In phantasy he could therefore produce children with his mother and no longer needed to put himself into the part of the baby.

These genital desires and phantasies, however, gave rise to various anxieties, and the attempt to solve his Oedipus conflicts by taking his father's place without having to fight him was only partially successful. Side by side with this relatively peaceful solution we find evidence in the drawing of Richard's fears that his father suspected his genital desires towards his mother, kept close watch over Richard and would castrate him. For when I had interpreted to Richard his reversal of the father-son situation, he told me that the plane on top was British and was patrolling. It will be remembered that the periscope of the submarine sticking into 'Rodney' represented Richard's wish for sexual intercourse with his mother. This implied that he was trying to oust his father and therefore expected his father to be suspicious of him. I then interpreted to him that he meant that his father was not only changed into a child, but was present as well in the rôle of the paternal super-ego, the father who watched him, tried to prevent him from having sexual intercourse with his mother and threatened him with punishment. (The patrolling aeroplane.)

I furthermore interpreted that Richard himself had been 'patrolling' his parents, for he was not only inquisitive about their sexual life but unconsciously strongly desired to interfere with it and to separate his parents.

Drawing IV illustrates the same material in a different way. While colouring the blue sections Richard had been singing the National Anthem, and he explained that his mother was the Queen and he was the King. Richard had become the father and had acquired the potent father genital. When he had finished the drawing and looked at it, he told me that there was 'plenty of Mum' and of himself in it and that they 'could really beat Dad'. He showed me that there was little of the bad father there (black). Since the father had been made into a harmless infant, there seemed to be no need to beat him. However, Richard had not much confidence in this omnipotent solution, as was shown by his saying that together with his mother he could beat his father if necessary. The lessening of anxiety had enabled him to face the rivalry with his father and even to fight with him.

While colouring the purple sections, Richard sang the Norwegian and Belgian anthems and said 'he's all right'. The smallness of the purple sections (in comparison with the blue and red) indicates that his brother too had been changed into a baby. The singing of the two anthems of small allied countries showed me that the 'he's all right' referred to both his father and brother, who had become

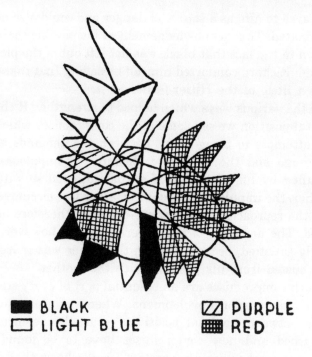

■ BLACK   **▨ PURPLE**
▢ LIGHT BLUE **▦ RED**

IV

harmless children. The repressed love for his father had at
this juncture of the analysis come more into the open.[1]
However, Richard felt he could not eliminate his father in
his dangerous aspects. Moreover, his own faeces—in so far
as they were unconsciously equated with the black father—

---

[1]It is significant that at the same time the libidinal desire for his
father's penis, which had been strongly repressed, also came up, and
in its most primary form. When looking again at the picture of the
monster against which the little man was fighting, Richard said: 'The
monster's awful to look at, but *its meat might be delicious* to eat.'

appeared to him as a source of danger and could also not be eliminated. This acknowledgement of his psychic reality is shown in the fact that black was not left out of the picture, though Richard comforted himself by saying that there was only a little of the Hitler-father in it.

In the various ways which helped to strengthen Richard's genital position we see some of the compromises which the ego attempts to bring about between the demands of the super-ego and the id. While Richard's id-impulses were gratified by his phantasy of sexual intercourse with his mother, the impulse to murder his father was circumvented and the reproaches of the super-ego were therefore diminished. The demands of the super-ego were, however, only partly satisfied, because though the father was spared, he was ousted from his position with the mother.

Such compromises are an essential part of every stage in the child's normal development. Whenever great fluctuations between libidinal positions occur, the defences are disturbed and new compromises have to be found. For instance, in the preceding section I have shown that, when Richard's oral anxieties were diminished, he attempted to cope with the conflict between his fears and desires by putting himself in phantasy into the rôle of an ideal baby who would not disturb the family peace. When the genital position was strengthened, however, and Richard could face his castration fear to a greater extent, a different compromise came about. Richard maintained his genital desires but avoided guilt by changing his father and brother into babies whom he would produce with his mother. Compromises of this kind at any stage of development can only bring about relative stability if the quantity of anxiety and guilt is not excessive in relation to the strength of the ego.

I have dealt in such details with the influence of anxiety and defences on genital development because it does not seem to me possible fully to understand sexual development without taking into account the fluctuations between the different stages of libidinal organization and the particular anxieties and defences which characterize those stages.

Anxieties relating to the internalized parents

Drawings V and *VI* need some introduction. Richard had developed a sore throat and a slight temperature the evening before, but nevertheless came to analysis, since it was warm summer weather. As I pointed out earlier, sore throats and colds were among his symptoms and, even when they were slight, gave rise in him to great hypochondriacal anxiety. At the beginning of the hour during which he made *Drawings V* and *VI* he was extremely anxious and worried. He told me that his throat felt very hot and that he had some poison behind his nose. His next association, produced with great resistance, was his fear that his food might be poisoned—a fear of which he had been conscious for years, though it was only with difficulty that, on this occasion as well as on former ones, he could bring it up in the analysis.

During this hour Richard frequently looked out of the window in a suspicious way. When he saw two men talking to each other, he said that they were spying on him. This was one of the repeated indications of his paranoid fears which related to his watching and persecuting father and brother, but above all centred on his parents in a secret and hostile alliance against him. In my interpretation I linked this suspicion with the fear of internal persecutors spying on him and plotting against him—an anxiety which had come up earlier in his analysis. A little later Richard suddenly put his finger as far down as he could into his throat and seemed very worried. He explained to me that he was looking for germs. I interpreted to him that the germs also stood for Germans (the black Hitler-father in unison with myself) and were in his mind connected with the two spying men, ultimately his parents. Thus the fear of germs was closely connected with his fear of being poisoned which unconsciously referred to his parents, though he did not consciously suspect them. The cold had stirred up these paranoid fears.

During this hour Richard had been making *Drawings V* and *VI*, and the only association I could get on that day was that *VI* was the same empire as *V*. In fact these two drawings were made on the same piece of paper.

On the following day Richard had completely recovered from his sore throat and appeared in a very different mood. He described vividly how much he had enjoyed his breakfast, particularly the shredded wheat, and showed me how he had munched it all up. (He had eaten very little during the previous two days.) His stomach, he said, had been quite small, thin and drawn in, and 'the big bones in it' had been 'sticking out' until he had his breakfast. These 'big bones' stood for his internalized father—or his father's genital—represented in earlier material at times by the monster, at times by the octopus. They expressed the bad aspect of his father's penis, while the 'delicious meat' of the monster expressed the desirable aspect of his father's penis. I interpreted the shredded wheat as standing for the good mother (the good breast and milk) since he had compared it on an earlier occasion to a bird's nest. Because his belief in the good internalized mother had increased, he felt less afraid of internal persecutors (the bones and the monster).

The analysis of the unconscious meaning of the sore throat had led to a diminution of anxieties with a corresponding change in the methods of defence. Richard's mood and associations during this hour clearly expressed this change. The world had suddenly become beautiful to him: he admired the countryside, my dress, my shoes, and said that I looked beautiful. He also spoke of his mother with great love and admiration. Thus, with the lessening of fears of internal persecutors, the external world appeared improved and more trustworthy to him and his capacity to enjoy it had increased. At the same time it was noticeable that his depression had given way to a hypomanic mood in which he denied his fears of persecution. In fact it was the lessening of anxiety which had allowed the manic defence against depression to come up. Richard's hypomanic mood did not, of course, last and in the further course of his analysis depression and anxiety appeared again and again.

I have so far mainly referred to Richard's relation to his mother as an external object. It had, however, become evident earlier in his analysis that the part she played as an external object was constantly interlinked with the part she played as an internal object. For the sake of clarity I have reserved this point to be illustrated by *Drawings V* and *VI,* which bring out vividly the rôle of the internalized parents in Richard's mental life.

In this hour Richard picked up *Drawings V* and *VI,* which he had made the day before, and freely associated to them. Now that his depression and hypochrondriacal anxieties had diminished, he was able to face the anxieties which had been underlying his depression. He pointed out to me that *V* looked like a bird and a 'very horrid' one. The light blue on top was a crown, the purple bit was the eye, and the beak was 'wide open'. This beak, as can be seen, was formed by the red and purple sections on the right, that is to say by the colours which always stood for himself and his brother.

I interpreted to him that the light-blue crown showed that the bird was his mother—the Queen, the ideal mother of former material—who now appeared as greedy and destructive. The fact that her beak was formed by red and purple sections expressed Richard's projection on to his mother of his own (as well as his brother's) oral-sadistic impulses.

V

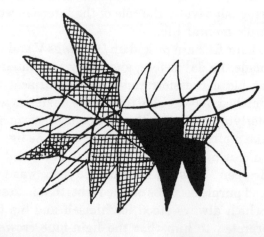

| ■ BLACK | ⊘ PURPLE |
| □ LIGHT BLUE | ▦ RED |

VI

It appears from this material that Richard had made important progress in the direction of facing his psychic reality, for he had become able to express the projection of his oral-sadistic and cannibalistic impulses on to his mother. Furthermore, as shown in *Drawing V*, he had allowed the 'good' and 'bad' aspects of the mother to come together more closely. The prototypes of these two aspects, usually kept more widely apart from each other, were the good, loved breast and the bad, hated breast. In fact, the defences by means of splitting and isolating can also be seen in this drawing, for the left-hand side of the picture is completely blue. On the right-hand side of *Drawing V*, however, the mother appears simultaneously as the 'horrid' bird (open beak) *and* as the queen (light-blue crown). With the lessening of denial of his psychic reality, Richard had also become more able to face external reality, for this made it possible for him to recognize the fact that his mother had actually frustrated him and had therefore aroused his hatred.

Following my interpretations of *Drawing V*, Richard repeated emphatically that the bird looked 'horrid' and gave some associations about *Drawing VI*. It, too, looked like a bird, he said, but without a head; and the black at the bottom of it was 'big job' dropping out from it. He said it was all 'very horrid'.

In my interpretation of *Drawing VI*, I reminded him that he had told me the day before that the two empires were the same. I suggested that *VI* represented himself, and that by internalizing the 'horrid bird' (*Drawing V*) he felt he had become like it. The open beak stood for his mother's greedy mouth, but also expressed his own desires to devour her, for the colours by which the beak was formed stood for himself and his brother (the greedy babies). In his mind he had devoured his mother as a destructive and devouring object. When in eating the breakfast food he had internalized the good mother, he felt that she was protecting him against the internalized bad father, the 'bones in his stomach'. When he internalized the 'horrid' bird mother he felt that she had become linked up with the monster father, and in his mind this terrifying combined parent figure was attacking him from within and eating him up as well as attacking him from without and castrating him.[1]

Thus Richard felt mutilated and castrated by the bad internal and external parents who retaliated for his attacks on them, and he expressed these fears in *Drawing VI*, for the bird appears there without a head. As a result of his oral-sadistic impulses towards his parents in the process of internalizing them, they had in his mind turned into correspondingly greedy and destructive enemies. Moreover, because he felt that by devouring his parents *he* had changed them into monster and bird, he experienced not only fear of these internalized persecutors but also guilt, all the more because he feared that he had exposed the good internal mother to the attacks of the internal monster. His guilt also related to his anal attacks on the external and internal parents which he had expressed by the 'horrid big job' dropping out of the bird.[2]

In the preceding hour, when Richard made these drawings, he had been so much under the sway of anxiety that he could not associate to them; now some relief of anxiety had made it possible for him to give associations.

An earlier drawing (*VII*) which expresses the internalization of his objects even more clearly than *Drawings V* and *VI* is of interest in this connection. When Richard finished this pattern drawing, he made a line round it and filled in the background with red. I found that this represented his

---

[1]It is relevant to recall here that he had been circumcised at the age of three and that ever since he had had a strong conscious fear of doctors and operations.

[2]Urethral impulses and anxieties were no less important in his phantasies, but do not specifically enter into this material.

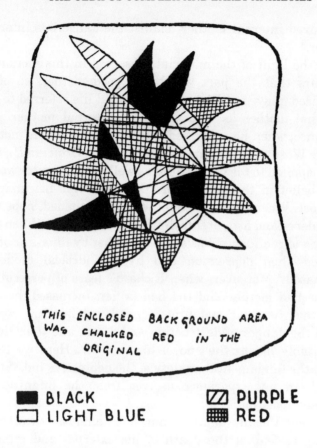

THIS ENCLOSED BACKGROUND AREA WAS CHALKED RED IN THE ORIGINAL

■■ BLACK   ▨ PURPLE
▢ LIGHT BLUE   ▦ RED

VII

'inside', containing his father, mother, brother and himself
in relation to each other. In his associations to this drawing
he expressed his satisfaction about the increase of the light
blue sections, *i.e.* his mother. He also spoke of his hope that
his brother would be his ally. His jealousy of his brother
often made him suspicious and frightened of his brother as a
rival. But at this moment he stressed the alliance with his
brother. Furthermore he pointed out that one of the black
sections was completely surrounded by his mother, brother
and himself. The implication was that he was allied with

the loved internal mother against the dangerous internal father.[1]

In the light of the material presented in this section, it appears that the part which the good mother, so often idealized, played in Richard's emotional life referred to the internal mother as well as to the external mother. For instance, when he expressed the hope that the blue mother in the West would extend her territory (cf. *Drawing II*), this hope applied to his inner world as well as to the outer world. The belief in the good internal mother was his greatest support. Whenever this belief was strengthened, hope and confidence and a greater feeling of security set in. When this feeling of confidence was shaken—either by illness or other causes—then depression and hypochondriacal anxieties increased.[2] Moreover, when Richard's fears of persecutors, of the bad mother and the bad father, increased, he also felt that he could not protect his loved internal objects from the danger of destruction and death; and their death inevitably meant the end of his own life. Here we touch upon the fundamental anxiety of the depressive individual, which in my experience derives from the infantile depressive position.

A significant detail from his analysis illustrates Richard's fear of the death of his external and internal objects. As I said earlier, his almost personal relation to the playroom was one of the characteristic features in the transference situation. After my journey to London, which

---

[1]This drawing also represented his mother's 'inside', where the same struggle was going on. Richard and his brother appeared in the rôle of her protective inner objects and his father as her dangerous inner object.

[2]There is little doubt that such anxieties are apt to turn to produce colds or other physical illnesses, or at least to lower the resistance to them. This means that we are here confronted with a vicious circle, because these illnesses in turn reinforced all his fears.

had strongly stirred up Richard's fear of air-raids and death, for some analytic sessions he could not bear having the electric stove turned off until the very moment when we left the house. In one of the hours which I had described in connection with the analysis of *Drawings III* and *IV* this obsession disappeared. In these hours, together with the strengthening of his genital desires and the diminution of anxiety and depression, the phantasy that he would be able to give 'good' babies to me and to his mother, and his love for babies, played a growing part in his associations. His obsessional insistence on keeping alight the stove in the room as long as possible was a measure of his depression.[1]

Summary of the boy's case history

Richard's failure to establish the genital position securely was largely caused by his incapacity to deal with anxiety in the early stages of his development. The great part which the bad breast played in Richard's emotional life was connected with his unsatisfactory feeding period and the strong oral-, urethral- and anal-sadistic impulses and phantasies which it stimulated. Richard's fears of the bad breast were to a certain extent counteracted by the idealization of the good breast, and in this way some of his love for his mother could be maintained. The bad qualities of the breast and his oral-sadistic impulses towards it were largely transferred to his father's penis. In addition, he experienced strong oral-sadistic impulses towards his father's penis, derived from jealousy and hatred in the early positive Oedipus situation. His father's genital therefore turned in his phantasy into a dangerous, biting and

---

[1]Keeping the stove alight also had the unconscious meaning of proving to himself that he was not castrated, and also that his father was not castrated.

poisonous object. The fear of the penis as an external and internal persecutor was so strong that trust in the good and productive qualities of the penis could not develop. In this way Richard's early feminine position was disturbed at the root by fears of persecution. These difficulties, experienced in the inverted Oedipus situation, interacted with the castration fear stimulated by his genital desires towards his mother. The hatred of his father which accompanied these desires, and expressed itself in the impulse to bite off his father's penis, led to the fear of being castrated in the same way, and therefore increased the repression of his genital desires.

One of the features of Richard's illness was a growing inhibition of all his activities and interests. This was linked with the severe repression of his aggressive tendencies, which was particularly marked in relation to his mother. In relation to his father and other men aggression was less repressed, though very much restrained by fear. Richard's predominant attitude to men was to pacify potential attackers and persecutors.

Richard's aggressiveness was least inhibited in relation to other children, though he was much too frightened to express it directly. His hatred of children, as well as his fear of them, was partly derived from the attitude towards his father's penis. The destructive penis and the destructive and greedy child who would exhaust the mother and ultimately destroy her were closely linked up with each other in his mind. For he unconsciously strongly maintained the equation 'penis = child'. He felt, too, that the *bad* penis could only produce *bad* children.

Another determining factor in his phobia of children was his jealousy of his brother and of any children his mother might have in the future. His unconscious sadistic attacks on the babies inside his mother's body were linked up with his hatred of his father's penis inside his mother. In one connection only could his love towards children show itself at times, and that was in a friendly attitude towards babies.

We know already that it was only by idealizing the mother–baby relationship that he could maintain his capacity for love. Because of his unconscious fear and guilt about his own oral-sadistic impulses, however, infants predominantly represented to him oral-sadistic beings. This was one of the reasons why he could not in phantasy fulfil his longing to give children to his mother. More fundamental still, oral anxiety had in his early development increased the fear connected with the aggressive aspects of the genital function and of his own penis. Richard's fear that his oral-sadistic impulses would dominate his genital desires and that his penis was a destructive organ was one of the main causes of his repression of his genital desires. Hence one essential means of making his mother happy, and making reparation for the babies which he felt he had destroyed, was barred to him. In all these various ways his oral-sadistic impulse, phantasies and fears interfered again and again with his genital development.

In the preceding sections I have referred repeatedly to the regression to the oral stage as a defence against the additional anxieties arising in the genital position; it is, however, important not to overlook the part played by fixation in these processes. Because his oral-, urethral- and anal-sadistic anxieties were excessive, fixation to these levels was very strong; in consequence, the genital organization was weak and the tendency to repression marked. However, in spite of his inhibitions, he had developed some sublimated genital trends. Moreover, in so far as his desires were predominantly directed towards his mother, and his feelings of jealousy and hatred towards his father, he had achieved some main features of the positive Oedipus situation and of heterosexual development. This picture was, however, in some ways deceptive since his love for his mother could only be maintained by reinforcing the oral elements in his relation to her and by idealizing the 'breast' mother. We have seen that in his drawings the blue sections always stood for his mother; this choice of colour was connected with his love of the cloudless blue sky and expressed his longing for an ideal bountiful breast which would never frustrate him.

The fact that Richard was thus enabled in some ways to keep alive his love for his mother had given him what little measure of stability he possessed, and had also allowed him to develop his heterosexual tendencies to a certain extent. It was obvious that anxiety and feelings of guilt entered largely into his fixation to his mother. Richard was very devoted to her, but in a rather infantile way. He could hardly bear to leave her out of sight and showed few signs of developing an independent and manly relation to her. His attitude towards other women—though far from being truly manly and independent—was in striking contrast to his great love and even blind admiration for his mother. His behaviour with women was very precocious, in some ways like that of a grown-up Don Juan. He tried to ingratiate himself in various ways, even by blatant flattery. At the same time he was often critical and contemptuous of women and amused if they were taken in by his flattery.

Here we see two contrasting attitudes to women which bring to mind some conclusions Freud has drawn. Speaking of the 'disunion between the tender and sensual currents of erotic feeling' in some men who suffer, as Freud describes it, from 'psychical impotence', *i.e.* who can only be potent under certain circumstances, he says: 'The whole sphere of love in such people remains divided in the two directions personified in art as sacred and profane (or animal) love. Where they love, they do not desire and where they desire they cannot love' (*S.E.* 11, p. 183).

There is an analogy between Freud's description and Richard's attitude to his mother. It was the 'genital' mother whom he feared and hated, while he turned his love and

tenderness towards the 'breast' mother. This division
between the two currents became apparent in the contrast
between his attitude to his mother and to other women.
While his genital desires towards his mother were strongly
repressed and she therefore remained an object of love and
admiration, these desires could become to some extent
active towards women other than his mother. But those
women were then objects of criticism and contempt to him.
They stood for the 'genital' mother, and it appeared that his
horror of genitality and his urge to repress it were reflected
in his contempt towards objects which aroused his genital
desires.

Among the anxieties which accounted for his fixation and
regression to the 'breast' mother, Richard's fear of his
mother's 'inside' as a place full of persecutors played a
predominant part. For the 'genital' mother, who was to him
the mother in sexual intercourse with the father, also
contained the 'bad' father's genital—or rather a multitude
of his genitals—thus forming a dangerous alliance with the
father against the son; she also contained the hostile babies.
In addition, there was the anxiety about his own penis as a
dangerous organ which would injure and damage his loved
mother.

The anxieties which disturbed Richard's genital development were closely linked with his relation to his parents as
internalized figures. To the picture of his mother's 'inside'
as a place of danger corresponded the feelings he had about
his own 'inside'. In previous sections we have seen that the
good mother (e.g. the good breakfast food) was protecting
him internally against the father, 'the long bones sticking
out' in his stomach. This picture of the mother protecting
him against the internalized father corresponded to the
mother-figure whom Richard felt urged to protect against
the bad father—a mother endangered by the oral and
genital attacks of the internal monster. Ultimately,
however, he felt her to be endangered by his own

oral-sadistic attacks on her. *Drawing II* showed the bad men
(his father, brother and himself) overwhelming and swal-
lowing up his mother. This fear derived from Richard's
fundamental feeling of guilt about having destroyed
(devoured) his mother and her breasts by his oral-sadistic
attacks in the process of internalizing her. In addition, he
expressed his guilt about his anal-sadistic attacks in
Drawing VI, for he pointed out the 'horrid big job' dropping
out from the bird. The equation between his own faeces and
the black Hitler-father became apparent earlier on in his
analysis when he began to make the empire drawings; for in
the earliest drawing Richard had introduced the black as
standing for himself, but soon decided that red stood for
himself and black for his father; he afterwards maintained
this arrangement throughout the drawings. This equation
was further illustrated by some of the associations to
Drawings V and *VI.* In *Drawing V* the black section
represented the bad father. In *Drawing VI* it represented
the 'horrid big job' dropping out of the mutilated bird.

To Richard's fear of his own destructiveness corresponded
the fear of his mother as a dangerous and retaliating object.
The 'horrid bird' with the open beak was a projection on to
his mother of his oral-sadistic impulses. Richard's actual
experiences of being frustrated by his mother could not by
themselves account for his having built up in his mind a
terrifying picture of an internal devouring mother. It
becomes clear in *Drawing VI* how very dangerous he felt the
'horrid' bird-mother to be. For the bird without a head
represented himself and corresponded to his fear of
castration by this dangerous mother united with the
monster father as external enemies. Moreover, in internal
situations he felt threatened by the alliance of the
internalized 'horrid' bird mother and the monster father.
These internal danger situations were the main cause of his
hypochondriacal and persecutory fears.

When Richard had become able during his analysis to face the psychological fact that his loved object was also his hated object and that the light-blue mother, the queen with the crown, was linked in his mind with the horrid bird with the beak, he could establish his love for his mother more securely. His feelings of love had become more closely linked with his feelings of hatred, and his happy experiences with his mother were no longer kept so widely apart from his experiences of frustration. He was therefore no longer driven on the one hand to idealize the good mother so strongly and on the other hand to form such a terrifying picture of the bad mother. Whenever he could allow himself to bring the two aspects of the mother together, this implied that the bad aspect was mitigated by the good one. This more secure good mother could then protect him against the 'monster' father. This again implied that at such times she was not felt to be so fatally injured by his oral greed and by the bad father, which in turn meant that he felt that both he and his father had become less dangerous. The good mother could come to life once more, and Richard's depression therefore lifted.

His increased hope of keeping the analyst and his mother alive as internal and external objects was bound up with the strengthening of his genital position and with a greater capacity to experience his Oedipus desires. Reproduction, the creation of good babies, which he unconsciously felt to be the most important means of combating death and the fear of death, had now become more possible to him in phantasy. Because he was less afraid of being carried away by his sadistic impulses, Richard believed that he would be able to produce good babies; for the creative and productive aspect of the male genital (his father's as well as his own) had come more strongly to the fore. The trust in his own constructive and reparative tendencies, as well as in his internal and external objects, had increased. His belief not only in the good mother but also in the good father had become strengthened. His father was no longer such a dangerous enemy that Richard could not face the fight with him as a hated rival. Thus he made an important step towards the strengthening of his genital position and towards facing the conflicts and fears bound up with his genital desires.

EXTRACTS FROM CASE HISTORY ILLUSTRATING THE GIRL'S OEDIPUS DEVELOPMENT

I have discussed some of the anxieties which disturb genital development in the boy and I shall now put forward some material from the case history of a little girl, Rita, which I have already described from various angles in earlier publications.[1] This material has certain advantages for purposes of presentation, for it is simple and straightforward. Most of this case material has been published previously; I shall however add a few details so far unpublished as well as some new interpretations which I could not have made at the time but which, in retrospect, seem to be fully borne out by the material.

My patient Rita, who was two years and nine months old at the beginning of her analysis, was a very difficult child to bring up. She suffered from anxieties of various kinds, from inability to tolerate frustration, and from frequent states of unhappiness. She showed marked obsessional features which had been increasing for some time, and she insisted on elaborate obsessional ceremonials. She alternated

[1]See [Klein, 1975] Lists of Patients at p. 444 ... and p. 292 of *Writings, 2 (The Psycho-Analysis of Children)*.

between an exaggerated 'goodness', accompanied by feelings of remorse, and states of 'naughtiness' when she
attempted to dominate everybody around her. She also had
difficulties over eating, was 'faddy', and frequently suffered
from loss of appetite. Though she was a very intelligent
child, the development and integration of her personality
were held back by the strength of her neurosis.

She often cried, apparently without cause, and when
asked by her mother why she was crying answered:
'Because I'm so sad.' To the question: 'Why are you so sad?'
she replied: 'Because I'm crying.' Her feelings of guilt and
unhappiness expressed themselves in constant questions to
her mother: 'Am I good?' 'Do you love me?' and so on. She
could not bear any reproach and, if reprimanded, either
burst into tears or became defiant. Her feeling of insecurity
in relation to her parents showed itself for instance in the
following incident from her second year. Once, so I was told,
she burst into tears because her father uttered a playful
threat against a bear in her picture book with whom she
had obviously identified herself.

Rita suffered from a marked inhibition in play. The only
thing she could do with her dolls, for instance, was to wash
them and change their clothes in a compulsive way. As soon
as she introduced any imaginative element, she had an
outbreak of anxiety and stopped playing.

The following are some relevant facts from her history.
Rita was breast-fed for a few months; then she had been
given the bottle, which she had at first been unwilling to
accept. Weaning from the bottle to solid food was again
troublesome, and she was still suffering from difficulties
over eating when I began her analysis. Moreover, at that
time she was still being given a bottle at night. Her mother
told me that she had given up trying to wean Rita from this
last bottle because every such attempt caused the child
great distress. With regard to Rita's habit training, which
was achieved early in her second year, I have reason to

assume that her mother had been rather too anxious over it. Rita's obsessional neurosis proved to be closely connected with her early habit training.

Rita shared her parents' bedroom until she was nearly two, and she repeatedly witnessed sexual intercourse between her parents. When she was two years old, her brother was born, and at that time her neurosis broke out in full force. Another contributory circumstance was the fact that her mother was herself neurotic and obviously ambivalent towards Rita.

Her parents told me that Rita was much more fond of her mother than of her father until the end of her first year. At the beginning of the second year she developed a marked preference for her father, together with pronounced jealousy of her mother. At fifteen months Rita repeatedly and unmistakably expressed the wish, when she sat on her father's knee, to be left alone with him in the room. She could already put this into words. At the age of about eighteen months there was a striking change, which showed itself in an altered relation to both her parents, as well as in various symptoms such as night terrors and animal phobias (particularly of dogs). Her mother once again became the favourite, yet the child's relation to her showed strong ambivalence. She clung to her mother so much that she could hardly let her out of her sight. This went together with attempts to dominate her and with an often unconcealed hatred of her. Concurrently Rita developed an outspoken dislike of her father.

These facts were clearly observed at the time and reported to me by her parents. In the case of older children, parents' reports about the earlier years are often unreliable, since, as time goes on, the facts are apt to be increasingly falsified in their memory. In Rita's case the details were still fresh in her parents' minds, and the analysis fully confirmed all the essentials of their report.

Early relations to the parents

At the beginning of Rita's second year some important elements of her Oedipus situation were plainly observable, such as her preference for her father and jealousy of her mother, and even the wish to take her mother's place with her father. In assessing Rita's Oedipus development in her second year we have to consider some outstanding external factors. The child shared her parents' bedroom and had ample opportunity for witnessing sexual intercourse between them; there was therefore a constant stimulus for libidinal desires and for jealousy, hatred and anxiety. When she was fifteen months old her mother became pregnant, and the child unconsciously understood her mother's condition; thus Rita's desire to receive a baby from her father, as well as her rivalry with her mother, was strongly reinforced. As a consequence, her aggressiveness, and the ensuing anxiety and feelings of guilt increased to such an extent that her Oedipus desires could not be maintained.

The difficulties in Rita's development cannot be explained, however, by these external stimuli alone. Many children are exposed to similar, and even to much more unfavourable, experiences without becoming seriously ill in consequence. We have therefore to consider the internal factors which, in interaction with the influences from without, led to Rita's illness and to the disturbance of her sexual development.

As the analysis revealed, Rita's oral-sadistic impulses were exceedingly strong and her capacity to tolerate tension of any kind was unusually low. These were some of the constitutional characteristics which determined her reactions to the early frustrations she suffered and from the beginning strongly affected her relation to her mother. When Rita's positive Oedipus desires came to the fore at the end of her first year, this new relation to both parents reinforced Rita's feelings of frustration, hatred and aggressiveness, with their concomitants of anxiety and guilt. She was unable to cope with these manifold conflicts and therefore could not maintain her genital desires.

Rita's relation to her mother was dominated by two great sources of anxiety: persecutory fear and depressive anxiety. In one aspect her mother represented a terrifying and retaliating figure. In another aspect she was Rita's indispensable loved and good object, and Rita felt her own aggression as a danger to this loved mother. She was therefore overwhelmed by the fear of losing her. It was the strength of these early anxieties and feelings of guilt which largely determined Rita's incapacity to tolerate the additional anxiety and guilt arising from the Oedipus feelings— rivalry and hatred against her mother. In defence she repressed her hatred and over-compensated for it by excessive love, and this necessarily implied a regression to earlier stages of the libido. Rita's relation to her father was also fundamentally influenced by these factors. Some of the resentment she felt towards her mother was deflected on to her father and reinforced the hatred of him which derived from the frustration of her Oedipus desires and which, towards the beginning of her second year, strikingly superseded her former love for her father. The failure to establish a satisfactory relation to her mother was repeated in her oral and genital relation to her father. Strong desires to castrate him (partly derived from frustration in the feminine position, partly from penis envy in the male position) became clear in the analysis.

Rita's sadistic phantasies were thus closely bound up with grievances derived from frustration in various libidinal positions and experienced in the inverted as well as in the positive Oedipus situation. The sexual intercourse between her parents played an important part in her sadistic phantasies and became in the child's mind a dangerous and frightening event, in which her mother appeared as the victim of her father's extreme cruelty. In consequence, not only did her father turn in her mind into someone dangerous to her mother but—in so far as Rita's Oedipus desires were maintained in identification with her mother—into a person dangerous towards herself. Rita's phobia of dogs went back to the fear of the dangerous penis of her father which would bite her in retaliation for her own impulses to castrate him. Her whole relation to her father was profoundly disturbed because he had turned into a 'bad man'. He was all the more hated because he became the embodiment of her own sadistic desires towards her mother.

The following episode, reported to me by her mother, illustrates this last point. At the beginning of her third year Rita was out for a walk with her mother and saw a cabman beating his horses cruelly. Her mother was extremely indignant, and the little girl also expressed strong indignation. Later on in the day she surprised her mother by saying: 'When are we going out again to see the bad man beating the horses?' thus revealing the fact that she had derived sadistic pleasure from the experience and wished for its repetition. In her unconscious the cabman represented her father and the horses her mother, and her father was carrying out in sexual intercourse the child's sadistic phantasies directed against her mother. The fear of her father's bad genital, together with the phantasy of her mother injured and destroyed by Rita's hatred and by the bad father—the cabman—interfered both with her positive and with her inverted Oedipus desires. Rita could neither identify herself with such a destroyed mother, nor allow herself to play in the homosexual position the rôle of the father. Thus in these early stages neither position could be satisfactorily established.

Some instances from the analytic material

The anxieties Rita experienced when she witnessed the primal scene are shown in the following material.

On one occasion during the analysis she put a triangular brick on one side and said: 'That's a little woman.' She then took a 'little hammer', as she called an oblong brick, and she hit the brick-box with it saying: 'When the hammer hit hard, the little woman was *so* frightened.' The triangular brick stood for herself, the 'hammer' for her father's penis, the box for her mother, and the whole situation represented her witnessing the primal scene. It is significant that she hit the box exactly in a place where it happened to be stuck together only with paper, so that she made a hole in it. This was one of the instances when Rita showed me symbolically her unconscious knowledge of the vagina and the part it played in her sexual theories.

The next two instances relate to her castration complex and penis envy. Rita was playing that she was travelling with her Teddy-bear to the house of a 'good' woman where she was to be given 'a marvellous treat'. This journey, however, did not go smoothly. Rita got rid of the engine-driver and took his place. But he came back again and again and threatened her, causing her great anxiety. An object of contention between her and him was her Teddy-bear whom she felt to be essential for the success of the journey. Here the bear represented her father's penis, and her rivalry with her father was expressed by this fight over the penis. She had robbed her father of it, partly from feelings of envy, hatred and revenge, partly in order to take his place with her mother and—by means of her father's potent penis—to make reparation for the injuries done to her mother in phantasy.

The next instance is linked with her bed-time ritual, which had become more and more elaborate and compulsive as time went on and involved a corresponding ceremonial with her doll. The main point of it was that she (and her doll as well) had to be tightly tucked up in the bed clothes, otherwise—as she said—a mouse or a 'butzen' (a word of her own) would get in through the window and bite off her own 'butzen'. The 'butzen' represented both her father's genital and her own: her father's penis would bite off her own imaginary penis just as *she* desired to castrate *him*. As I see it now, the fear of her mother attacking the 'inside' of her body also contributed to her fear of someone coming through the window. The room also represented her body and the assailant was her mother retaliating for the child's attacks on her. The obsessional need to be tucked in with such elaborate care was a defence against all these fears.

Super-ego development

The anxieties and feelings of guilt described in the last two sections were bound up with Rita's super-ego development. I found in her a cruel and unrelenting super-ego, such as underlies severe obsessional neuroses in adults. This development I could in the analysis trace back definitely to the beginning of her second year. In the light of my later experience I am bound to conclude that the beginnings of Rita's super-ego reached back to the first few months of life.

In the travelling game I have described, the engine-driver represented her super-ego as well as her actual father. We also see her super-ego at work in Rita's obsessional play with her doll, when she went through a ritual similar to her own bed-time ceremonial, putting the doll to sleep and tucking her up very elaborately. Once during the analysis Rita placed an elephant by the doll's bedside. As she explained, the elephant was to prevent the 'child' (doll) from getting up, because otherwise the 'child' would steal into its parents' bedroom and either 'do them some harm or take something away from them'. The elephant represented her super-ego (her father and mother), and the attacks on her parents which it was to prevent were the expression of Rita's own sadistic impulses centring on her parents' sexual intercourse and her mother's pregnancy. The super-ego was to make it impossible for the child to rob her mother of the baby inside her, to injure or destroy her mother's body, as well as to castrate the father.

A significant detail from her history was that early in her third year Rita repeatedly declared, when she was playing with dolls, that she *was not the doll's mother*. In the context of the analysis it appeared that she could not allow herself to be the doll's mother because the doll stood for her baby brother whom she wanted and feared to take away from her mother. Her guilt also related to her aggressive phantasies during her mother's pregnancy. When Rita could not play at being her doll's mother, this inhibition derived from her feelings of guilt as well as from her fear of a cruel mother-figure, infinitely more severe than her actual mother had ever been. Not only did Rita see her *real* mother in this distorted light, but she felt in constant danger from a terrifying *internal* mother-figure. I have referred to Rita's phantasied attacks on her mother's body and the corresponding anxiety that her mother would attack her and rob her of her imaginary babies, as well as to her fear of being attacked and castrated by her father. I would now go further in my interpretations. To the phantasied attacks on her body by her parents as external figures corresponded fear of inner attacks by the internalized persecuting parent-figures who formed the cruel part of her super-ego.[1]

[1] In my General Theoretical Summary below I deal with the girl's super-ego development and the essential part the good internalized father plays in it. With Rita this aspect of her super-ego formation had not appeared in her analysis. A development in this direction, however, was indicated by the improved relation to her father towards the end of her analysis. As I see it now, the anxiety and guilt relating to her mother so much dominated her emotional life that both the relation to the external father and to the internalized father-figure were interfered with.

The harshness of Rita's super-ego often showed in her play during the analysis. For instance, she used to punish her doll cruelly; then would follow an outbreak of rage and fear. She was identified both with the harsh parents who inflict severe punishment and with the child who is being cruelly punished and bursts into a rage. This was not only noticeable in her play but in her behaviour in general. At certain times she seemed to be the mouthpiece of a severe and unrelenting mother, at other times of an uncontrollable, greedy and destructive infant. There seemed to be very little of her own ego to bridge these two extremes and to modify the intensity of the conflict. The gradual process of integration of her super-ego was severely interfered with, and she could not develop an individuality of her own.

Persecutory and depressive anxieties disturbing the Oedipus development

Rita's depressive feelings were a marked feature in her neurosis. Her states of sadness and crying without cause, her constant questions whether her mother loved her—all these were indications of her depressive anxieties. These anxieties were rooted in her relation to her mother's breasts. In consequence of her sadistic phantasies, in which she had attacked the breast and her mother as a whole, Rita was dominated by fears which profoundly influenced her relation to her mother. In one aspect she loved her mother as a good and indispensable object and felt guilty because she had endangered her by her aggressive phantasies; in another aspect she hated and feared her as the bad, persecutory mother (in the first place, the bad breast). These fears and complex feelings, which related to her mother both as an external and internal object, constituted her infantile depressive position. Rita was incapable of dealing with these acute anxieties and could not overcome her depressive position.

In this connection some material from the early part of her analysis is significant.[1] She scribbled on a piece of paper and blackened it with great vigour. Then she tore it up and threw the scraps into a glass of water which she put to her mouth as if to drink from it. At that moment she stopped and said under her breath: 'Dead woman.' This material, with the same words, was repeated on another occasion.

The piece of paper blackened, torn up and thrown into the water represented her mother destroyed by oral, anal and urethral means, and this picture of a dead mother related not only to the external mother when she was out of sight but also to the *internal* mother. Rita had to give up the rivalry with her mother in the Oedipus situation because her unconscious fear of loss of the internal and external object acted as a barrier to every desire which would increase her hatred of her mother and therefore cause her mother's death. These anxieties, derived from the oral position, underlay the marked depresssion which Rita developed at her mother's attempt to wean her of the last bottle. Rita would not drink the milk from a cup. She fell into a state of despair; she lost her appetite in general, refused food, clung more than ever to her mother, asking her again and again whether she loved her, if she had been naughty, and so on. Her analysis revealed that the weaning represented a cruel punishment for her aggressive desires and death wishes against her mother. Since the loss of the bottle stood for the final loss of the breast, Rita felt when the bottle was taken away that she had actually destroyed her mother. Even the presence of her mother could do no more than temporarily alleviate these fears. The inference suggests itself that while the lost bottle represented the lost good breast, the cup of milk which Rita refused in her state of depression following the weaning represented the de-

---

[1]This piece of material has not appeared in former publications.

stroyed and dead mother, just as the glass of water with the torn paper had represented the 'dead woman'.

As I have suggested, Rita's depressive anxieties about the death of her mother were bound up with persecutory fears relating to attacks on her own body by a retaliating mother. In fact such attacks always appear to a girl not only as a danger to her body, but as a danger to everything precious which in her mind her 'inside' contains: her potential children, the good mother and the good father.

The incapacity to protect these loved objects against external and internal persecutors is part of the most fundamental anxiety situation of girls.[1]

Rita's relation to her father was largely determined by the anxiety situations centring on her mother. Much of her hatred and fear of the bad breast had been transferred to her father's penis. Excessive guilt and fear of loss relating to her mother had also been transferred to her father. All this—together with the frustration suffered directly from her father—had interfered with the development of her positive Oedipus complex.

Her hatred of her father was reinforced by penis envy and by rivalry with him in the inverted Oedipus situation. Her attempts to cope with her penis envy led to a reinforced belief in her imaginary penis. However, she felt this penis to be endangered by a bad father who would castrate her in retaliation for her own desires to castrate him. When Rita was afraid of her father's 'butzen' coming into the room and biting off her own 'butzen', this was an instance of her castration fear.

Her desires to annex her father's penis and to play his part with her mother were clear indications of her penis

[1]This anxiety situation entered to some extent into Rita's analysis, but at that time I did not realize fully the importance of such anxieties and their close connection with depression. This became clearer to me in the light of later experience.

envy. This was illustrated by the play material I have quoted: she travelled with her Teddy-bear, representing the penis, to the 'good woman' who was to give them a 'marvellous treat'. The wish to possess a penis of her own, however, was—as her analysis showed me—strongly rein-forced by anxieties and guilt relating to the death of her loved mother. These anxieties, which early on had under-mined her relation to her mother, largely contributed to the failure of the positive Oedipus development. They also had the effect of reinforcing Rita's desires to possess a penis, for she felt that she could only repair the damage done to her mother, and make up for the babies which in phantasy she had taken from her, if she possessed a penis of her own with which to gratify her mother and give her children.

Rita's excessive difficulties in dealing with her inverted and positive Oedipus complex were thus rooted in her depressive position. Along with the lessening of these anxieties, she became able to tolerate her Oedipus desires and to achieve increasingly a feminine and maternal attitude. Towards the end of her analysis, which was cut short owing to external circumstances, Rita's relation to both parents, as well as to her brother, improved. Her aversion to her father, which had until then been very marked, gave place to affection for him; the ambivalence towards her mother decreased, and a more friendly and stable relationship developed.

Rita's changed attitude towards her Teddy-bear and her doll reflected the extent to which her libidinal development had progressed and her neurotic difficulties and the severity of her super-ego had been reduced. Once, near the end of the analysis, while she was kissing the bear and hugging it and calling it pet names, she said: 'I'm not a bit unhappy any more because now I've got such a dear little baby.' She could now allow herself to be the mother of her imaginary child. This change was not an altogether new development, but in some measure a return to an earlier libidinal position. In her second year Rita's desires to receive her father's penis and to have a child from him had been disturbed by anxiety and guilt relating to her mother; her positive Oedipus development broke down and there was a marked aggravation of her neurosis. When Rita said emphatically that she was not the mother of her doll, she clearly indicated the struggle against her desires to have a baby. Under the stress of her anxiety and guilt she could not maintain the feminine position and was driven to reinforce the male position. The bear thus came to stand predominantly for the desired penis. Rita could not allow herself the wish for a child from her father, and the identification with her mother in the Oedipus situation could not be established, until her anxieties and guilt in relation to both parents had lessened.

GENERAL THEORETICAL SUMMARY

(a) Early stages of the Oedipus complex in both sexes

The clinical pictures of the two cases I have presented in this paper differed in many ways. However, the two cases had some important features in common, such as strong oral-sadistic impulses, excessive anxiety and guilt, and a low capacity of the ego to tolerate tension of any kind. In my experience, these are some of the factors which, in interaction with external circumstances, prevent the ego from gradually building up adequate defences against anxiety. As a result, the working through of early anxiety situations is impaired and the child's emotional, libidinal and ego-development suffers. Owing to the dominance of anxiety and guilt there is an over-strong fixation to the early stages of libidinal organization and, in interaction with this, an excessive tendency to regress to those early stages. In consequence, the Oedipus development is interfered with and the genital organization cannot be securely established. In the two cases referred to in this paper, as well as in others, the Oedipus complex began to develop on normal lines when these early anxieties were diminished.

The effect of anxiety and guilt on the course of the Oedipus development is to some extent illustrated by the two brief case histories I have given. The following survey of my theoretical conclusions on certain aspects of the Oedipus development is, however, based on the whole of my analytic work with child and adult cases, ranging from normality to severe illness.

A full description of the Oedipus development would have to include a discussion of external influences and experiences at every stage, and of their effect throughout childhood. I have deliberately sacrificed the exhaustive description of external factors to the need to clarify the most important issues.[1]

My experience has led me to believe that, from the very beginning of life, libido is fused with aggressiveness, and that the development of the libido is at every stage vitally affected by anxiety derived from aggressiveness. Anxiety, guilt and depressive feelings at times drive the libido forward to new sources of gratification, at times they check the development of the libido by reinforcing the fixation to an earlier object and aim.

In comparison with the later phases of the Oedipus complex, the picture of its earliest stages is necessarily

---

[1]My main purpose in this summary is to provide a clear presentation of my views on some aspects of the Oedipus complex. I also intend to compare my conclusions with certain of Freud's statements on the subject. I find it impossible, therefore, at the same time to quote other authors or to make references to the copious literature dealing with this subject. With regard to the girl's Oedipus complex, however, I should like to draw attention to chapter xi in my book, *The Psycho-Analysis of Children* (1932), in which I have referred to the views of various authors on this subject.

more obscure, as the infant's ego is immature and under the full sway of unconscious phantasy; also his instinctual life is in its most polymorphous phase. These early stages are characterized by swift fluctuations between different objects and aims, with corresponding fluctuations in the nature of the defences. In my view, the Oedipus complex starts during the first year of life and in both sexes develops to begin with on similar lines. The relation to the mother's breast is one of the essential factors which determine the whole emotional and sexual development. I therefore take the breast relation as my starting point in the following description of the beginnings of the Oedipus complex in both sexes.

It seems that the search for new sources of gratification is inherent in the forward movement of the libido. The gratification experienced at the mother's breast enables the infant to turn his desires towards new objects, first of all towards his father's penis. Particular impetus, however, is given to the new desire by frustration in the breast relation. It is important to remember that frustration depends on internal factors as well as on actual experiences. Some measure of frustration at the breast is inevitable, even under the most favourable conditions, for what the infant actually desires is *unlimited* gratification. The frustration experienced at the mother's breast leads both boy and girl to turn away from it and stimulates the infant's desire for oral gratification from the penis of the father. The breast and the penis are, therefore, the primary objects of the infant's oral desires.[1]

[1]In dwelling on the infant's fundamental relation to the mother's breast and to the father's penis, and on the ensuing anxiety situations and defences, I have in mind more than the relation to part-objects. In fact these part-objects are from the beginning associated in the infant's mind with his mother and father. Day-to-day experiences with his parents, and the unconscious relation which develops to them as inner objects, come increasingly to cluster round these primary part-objects and add to their prominence in the child's unconscious.

Frustration and gratification from the outset mould the infant's relation to a loved good breast and to a hated bad breast. The need to cope with frustration and with the ensuing aggression is one of the factors which lead to idealizing the good breast and good mother, and correspondingly to intensifying the hatred and fears of the bad breast and bad mother, which becomes the prototype of all persecuting and frightening objects.

The two conflicting attitudes to the mother's breast are carried over into the new relation to the father's penis. The frustration suffered in the earlier relation increases the demands and hopes from the new source and stimulates love for the new object. The inevitable disappointment in the new relation reinforces the pull-back to the first object; and this contributes to the lability and fluidity of emotional attitudes and of the stages of libidinal organization.

Furthermore, aggressive impulses, stimulated and reinforced by frustration, turn, in the child's mind, the victims of his aggressive phantasies into injured and retaliating figures which threaten him with the same sadistic attacks as he commits against the parents in phantasy.[1] In consequence, the infant feels an increased need for a loved and loving object—a perfect, an ideal object—in order to satisfy his craving for help and security. Each object, therefore, is in turn liable to become at times good, at times bad. This movement to and fro between the various aspects of the primary imagos implies a close interaction between the early stages of the inverted and positive Oedipus complex.

---

[1]Allowance must be made for the great difficulty of expressing a young child's feelings and phantasies in adult language. All descriptions of early unconscious phantasies—and for that matter of unconscious phantasies in general—can therefore only be considered as pointers to the contents rather than to the form of such phantasies.

Since under the dominance of the oral libido the infant from the beginning introjects his objects, the primary imagos have a counterpart in his inner world. The imagos of his mother's breast and of his father's penis are established within his ego and form the nucleus of his super-ego. To the introjection of the good and bad breast and mother corresponds the introjection of the good and bad penis and father. They become the first representatives on the one hand of protective and helpful internal figures, on the other hand of retaliating and persecuting internal figures, and are the first identifications which the ego develops.

The relation to internal figures interacts in manifold ways with the child's ambivalent relation to both parents as external objects. For to the introjection of external objects corresponds at every step the projection of internal figures on to the external world, and this interaction underlies the relation to the actual parents as well as the development of the super-ego. In consequence of this interaction, which implies an orientation outwards and inwards, there is a constant fluctuation between internal and external objects and situations. These fluctuations are bound up with the movement of the libido between different aims and objects, and thus the course of the Oedipus complex and the development of the super-ego are closely interlinked.

Though still overshadowed by oral, urethral and anal libido, genital desires soon mingle with the child's oral impulses. Early genital desires, as well as oral ones, are directed towards mother and father. This is in line with my assumption that in both sexes there is an inherent unconscious knowledge of the existence of the penis as well as of the vagina. In the male infant, genital sensations are the basis for the expectation that his father possesses a penis which the boy desires according to the equation 'breast = penis'. At the same time, his genital sensations and impulses also imply the search for an opening into which to insert his penis, *i.e.* they are directed towards his mother. The infant girl's genital sensations correspondingly prepare the desire to receive her father's penis into her vagina. It appears therefore that the genital desires for the penis of the father, which mingle with oral desires, are at the root of the early stages of the girl's positive and of the boy's inverted Oedipus complex.

The course of libidinal development is at every stage influenced by anxiety, guilt and depressive feelings. In the two earlier papers I have repeatedly referred to the infantile depressive position as the central position in early development. I would now rather suggest the following formulation: the core of infantile depressive feelings, *i.e.* the child's fear of the loss of his loved objects, as a consequence of his hatred and aggression, enters into his object relations and Oedipus complex from the beginning.

An essential corollary of anxiety, guilt and depressive feelings is the urge for reparation. Under the sway of guilt the infant is impelled to undo the effect of his sadistic impulses by libidinal means. Thus feelings of love, which co-exist with aggressive impulses, are reinforced by the drive for reparation. Reparative phantasies represent, often in minute detail, the obverse of sadistic phantasies, and to the feeling of sadistic omnipotence corresponds the feeling of reparative omnipotence. For instance, urine and faeces represent agents of destruction when the child hates and gifts when he loves; but when he feels guilty and driven to make reparation, the 'good' excrements in his mind become the means by which he can cure the damage done by his 'dangerous' excrements. Again, both boy and girl, though in different ways, feel that the penis which damaged and destroyed the mother in their sadistic phantasies becomes the means of restoring and curing her in phantasies of reparation. The desire to give and receive libidinal gratification is thus enhanced by the drive for reparation. For the infant feels that in this way the injured object can be restored, and also that the power of his aggressive impulses is diminished, that his impulses of love are given free rein, and guilt is assuaged.

The course of libidinal development is thus at every step stimulated and reinforced by the drive for reparation, and ultimately by the sense of guilt. On the other hand, guilt which engenders the drive for reparation also inhibits libidinal desires. For when the child feels that his aggressiveness predominates, libidinal desires appear to him as a danger to his loved objects and must therefore be repressed.

(b) The boy's Oedipus development

So far I have outlined the early stages of the Oedipus complex in both sexes, and I shall now deal particularly with the boy's development. His feminine position—which vitally influences his attitude to both sexes—is arrived at under the dominance of oral, urethral and anal impulses and phantasies and is closely linked with his relation to his mother's breasts. If the boy can turn some of his love and libidinal desires from his mother's breast towards his father's penis, while retaining the breast as a good object, then his father's penis will figure in his mind as a good and creative organ which will give him libidinal gratification as well as give him children as it does to his mother. These feminine desires are always an inherent feature in the boy's development. They are at the root of his inverted Oedipus complex and constitute the first homosexual position. The reassuring picture of his father's penis as a good and creative organ is also a precondition for the boy's capacity to develop his positive Oedipus desires. For only if the boy has a strong enough belief in the 'goodness' of the male genital—his father's as well as his own—can he allow himself to experience his genital desires towards his

mother. When his fear of the castrating father is mitigated
by trust in the good father, he can face his Oedipus hatred
and rivalry. Thus the inverted and positive Oedipus
tendencies develop simultaneously, and there is a close
interaction between them.

There are good grounds for assuming that as soon as
genital sensations are experienced, castration fear is
activated. Castration fear in the male, according to Freud's
definition, is the fear of having the genital attacked, injured
or removed. In my view this fear is first of all experienced
under the dominance of oral libido. The boy's oral-sadistic
impulses towards his mother's breast are transferred to his
father's penis, and in addition rivalry and hatred in the
early Oedipus situation find expression in the boy's desire to
bite off his father's penis. This arouses his fear that his own
genital will be bitten off by his father in retaliation.

There are a number of early anxieties from various
sources which contribute to castration fear. The boy's
genital desires towards his mother are from the beginning
fraught with phantastic dangers because of his oral,
urethral and anal phantasies of attack on the mother's
body. The boy feels that her 'inside' is injured, poisoned and
poisonous; it also contains in his phantasy his father's penis
which—owing to his own sadistic attacks on it—is felt as a
hostile and castrating object and threatens his own penis
with destruction.

To this frightening picture of his mother's 'inside'—which
co-exists with the picture of his mother as a source of all
goodness and gratification—correspond fears about the
inside of his own body. Outstanding among these is the
infant's fear of internal attack by a dangerous mother,
father or combined parental figure in retaliation for his own
aggressive impulses. Such fears of persecution decisively
influence the boy's anxieties about his own penis. For every
injury done to his 'inside' by internalized persecutors

implies to him an attack too on his own penis, which he fears will be mutilated, poisoned or devoured from within. It is, however, not only his penis he feels he must preserve, but also the good contents of his body, the good faeces and urine, the babies which he wishes to grow in the feminine position and the babies which—in identification with the good and creative father—he wishes to produce in the male position. At the same time he feels impelled to protect and preserve the loved objects which he internalized simultaneously with the persecuting figures. In these ways the fear of internal attacks on his loved objects is closely linked with castration fear and reinforces it.

Another anxiety contributory to castration fear derives from the sadistic phantasies in which his excrements have turned poisonous and dangerous. His own penis too, which is equated with these dangerous faeces, and in his mind is filled with bad urine, becomes therefore in his phantasies of copulation an organ of destruction. This fear is increased by the belief that he contains the bad penis of his father, *i.e.* by an identification with the bad father. When this particular identification gains in strength, it is experienced as an alliance with the bad internal father against his mother. In consequence, the boy's belief in the productive and reparative quality of his genital is diminished; he feels that his own aggressive impulses are reinforced and that the sexual intercourse with his mother would be cruel and destructive.

Anxieties of this nature have an important bearing on his actual castration fear and on the repression of his genital desires, as well as on the regression to earlier stages. If these various fears are excessive and the urge to repress genital desires is over-strong, difficulties in potency are bound to arise later. Normally such fears in the boy are counteracted by the picture of his mother's body as the source of all goodness (good milk and babies) as well as by his introjection of loved objects. When his love impulses predominate, the products and contents of his body take on the significance of gifts; his penis becomes the means of giving gratification and children to his mother and of making reparation. Also, if the feeling of containing the good breast of his mother and the good penis of his father has the upper hand, the boy derives from this a strengthened trust in himself which allows him to give freer rein to his impulses and desires. In union and identification with the good father he feels that his penis acquires reparative and creative qualities. All these emotions and phantasies enable him to face his castration fear and to establish the genital position securely. They are also the precondition for sublimated potency, which has an important bearing on the child's activities and interest; and at the same time the foundation is laid for the achievement of potency in later life.

(c) The girl's Oedipus development

I have already described the early stages of the girl's Oedipus development in so far as it is in line with the boy's development. I shall now point out some essential features which are specific to the girl's Oedipus complex.

When genital sensations in the infant girl gain in strength, in keeping with the receptive nature of her genitals, the desire to receive the penis arises.[1] At the same time she has an unconscious knowledge that her body contains potential children whom she feels to be her most

[1] The analysis of young children leaves no doubt as to the fact that the vagina is represented in the unconscious of the child. Actual vaginal masturbation in early childhood is much more frequent than has been assumed, and this is corroborated by a number of authors.

precious possession. The penis of her father as the giver of children, and equated to children, becomes the object of great desire and admiration for the little girl. This relation to the penis as a source of happiness and good gifts is enhanced by the loving and grateful relation to the good breast.

Together with the unconscious knowledge that she contains potential babies, the little girl has grave doubts as to her future capacity to bear children. On many grounds she feels at a disadvantage in comparison with her mother. In the child's unconscious the mother is imbued with magic power, for all goodness springs from her breast and the mother also contains the father's penis and the babies. The little girl—in contrast to the boy, whose hope for potency gains strength from the possession of a penis which can be compared with his father's penis—has no means of reassuring herself about her future fertility. In addition, her doubts are increased by all the anxieties relating to the contents of her body. These anxieties intensify the impulses to rob her mother's body of her children as well as of the father's penis, and this in turn intensifies the fear lest her own inside be attacked and robbed of its 'good' contents by a retaliating external and internal mother.

Some of these elements are operative in the boy as well, but the fact that the girl's genital development centres on the feminine desire to receive her father's penis and that her main unconscious concern is for her imaginary babies, is a specific feature of the girl's development. In consequence, her phantasies and emotions are predominantly built round her inner world and inner objects; her Oedipus rivalry expresses itself essentially in the impulse to rob her mother of the father's penis and the babies; the fear of having her body attacked and her inner good objects injured or taken away by a bad retaliating mother plays a prominent and lasting part in her anxieties. This, as I see it, is the leading anxiety situation of the girl.

Moreover, while in the boy the envy of his mother (who is felt to contain the penis of his father and the babies) is an element in his inverted Oedipus complex, with the girl this envy forms part of her positive Oedipus situation. It remains an essential factor throughout her sexual and emotional development, and has an important effect on her identification with her mother in the sexual relation with the father as well as in the maternal rôle.

The girl's desire to possess a penis and to be a boy is an expression of her bisexuality and is as inherent a feature in girls as the desire to be a woman is in boys. Her wish to have a penis of her own is secondary to her desire to receive the penis, and is greatly enhanced by the frustrations in her feminine position and by the anxiety and guilt experienced in the positive Oedipus situation. The girl's penis envy covers in some measure the frustrated desire to take her mother's place with the father and to receive children from him.

I can here only touch upon the specific factors which underlie the girl's super-ego formation. Because of the great part her inner world plays in the girl's emotional life, she has a strong urge to fill this inner world with good objects. This contributes to the intensity of her introjective processes, which are also reinforced by the receptive nature of her genital. The admired internalized penis of her father forms an intrinsic part of her super-ego. She identifies herself with her father in her male position, but this identification rests on the possession of an imaginary penis. Her main identification with her father is experienced in relation to the internalized penis of her father, and this relation is based on the feminine as well as on the male position. In the feminine position she is driven by her sexual desires, and by her longing for a child, to internalize her father's penis. She is capable of complete submission to this admired internalized father, while in the male position she wishes to emulate him in all her masculine aspirations and sublimations. Thus her male identification with her father is mixed with her feminine attitude, and it is this combination which characterizes the feminine super-ego.

To the admired good father in the girl's super-ego formation corresponds to some extent the bad castrating father. Her main anxiety object, however, is the persecuting mother. If the internalization of a good mother, with whose maternal attitude she can identify herself, counterbalances this persecutory fear, her relation to the good internalized father becomes strengthened by her own maternal attitude towards him.

In spite of the prominence of the inner world in her emotional life, the little girl's need for love and her relation to people show a great dependence on the outer world. This contradiction is, however, only apparent, because this dependence on the outer world is reinforced by her need to gain reassurance about her inner world.

(d) Some comparisons with the classical concept of the Oedipus complex

I now propose to compare my views with those of Freud on certain aspects of the Oedipus complex, and to clarify some divergences to which my experience has led me. Many aspects of the Oedipus complex, on which my work fully confirms Freud's findings, have been to some extent implied in my description of the Oedipus situation. The magnitude of the subject, however, makes it necessary for me to refrain from discussing these aspects in detail, and I have to limit myself to clarifying some of the divergences. The following summary represents in my opinion the essence of Freud's conclusions about certain essential features of the Oedipus development.[1]

According to Freud, genital desires emerge and a definite object choice takes place during the phallic phase, which extends from about three to five years of age, and is contemporaneous with the Oedipus complex. During this phase '. . . only one genital, namely the male one, comes into account. What is present, therefore, is not a primacy of the genitals, but a primacy of the phallus' (*S.E.* **19**, p. 142).

In the boy, 'what brings about the destruction of the child's phallic organization is the threat of castration' (*S.E.* **19**, p. 175). Furthermore, his super-ego, the heir of the Oedipus complex, is formed by the internalization of the parental authority. Guilt is the expression of tension between the ego and the super-ego. It is only when the super-ego has developed that the use of the term 'guilt' is justified. Predominant weight is given by Freud to the boy's super-ego as the internalized authority of the father; and, though in some measure he acknowledges the identification with the mother as a factor in the boy's super-ego formation, he has not expressed his views on this aspect of the super-ego in any detail.

With regard to the girl, in Freud's view her long 'pre-Oedipal attachment' to her mother covers the period before she enters the Oedipus situation. Freud also characterizes this period as 'the phase of exclusive attachment to the mother, which may be called the pre-Oedipus

[1]This summary is mainly derived from the following of Freud's writings: *The Ego and the Id (S.E.* **19**), 'The Infantile Genital Organization' (*S.E.* **19**), 'The Dissolution of the Oedipus Complex' (*S.E.* **19**), 'Some Psychical Consequences of the Anatomical Distinction between the Sexes' (*S.E.* **19**), 'Female Sexuality' (*S.E.* **21**) and *New Introductory Lectures (S.E.* **22**).

phase' (*S.E.* **21,** p. 230). Subsequently during her phallic phase, the girl's fundamental desires in relation to her mother, maintained with the greatest intensity, focus on receiving a penis from her. The clitoris represents in the little girl's mind her penis, clitoris masturbation is the expression of her phallic desires. The vagina is not yet discovered and will only play its part in womanhood. When the girl discovers that she does not possess a penis, her castration complex comes to the fore. At this juncture the attachment to her mother is broken off with resentment and hatred because her mother has not given her a penis. She also discovers that even her mother lacks a penis, and this contributes to her turning away from her mother to her father. She first turns to her father with the wish to receive a penis, and only subsequently with the desire to receive a child from him, 'that is, a baby takes the place of a penis in accordance with an ancient symbolic equivalence' (*S.E.* **22,** p. 128). In these ways her Oedipus complex is ushered in by her castration complex.

The girl's main anxiety situation is the loss of love, and Freud connects this fear with the fear of the death of her mother.

The girl's super-ego development differs in various ways from the boy's super-ego development, but they have in common an essential feature, *i.e.* that the super-ego and the sense of guilt are sequels to the Oedipus complex.

Freud refers to the girl's motherly feelings derived from the early relation to her mother in the pre-Oedipal phase. He also refers to the girl's identification with her mother, derived from her Oedipus complex. But he has not linked these two attitudes, nor shown how the feminine identification with her mother in the Oedipus situation affects the course of the girl's Oedipus complex. In his view, while the girl's genital organization is taking shape, she values her mother predominantly in the phallic aspect.

I shall now summarize my own views on these essential issues. As I see it, the boy's and girl's sexual and emotional development *from early infancy onwards* includes genital sensations and trends, which constitute the first stages of the inverted and positive Oedipus complex; they are experienced under the primacy of oral libido and mingle with urethral and anal desires and phantasies. The libidinal stages overlap from the earliest months of life onwards. The positive and inverted Oedipus tendencies are from their inception in close interaction. It is during the stage of genital primacy that the positive Oedipus situation reaches its climax.

In my view, infants of both sexes experience genital desires directed towards their mother and father, and they have an unconscious knowledge of the vagina as well as of the penis.[1] For these reasons Freud's earlier term 'genital phase' seems to me more adequate than his later concept of the 'phallic phase'.

The super-ego in both sexes comes into being during the oral phase. Under the sway of phantasy life and of conflicting emotions, the child at every stage of libidinal organization introjects his objects—primarily his parents— and builds up the super-ego from these elements.

Thus, though the super-ego corresponds in many ways to the actual people in the young child's world, it has various components and features which reflect the phantastic images in his mind. All the factors which have a bearing on his object relations play a part from the beginning in the building-up of the super-ego.

---

[1]This knowledge exists side by side with the infant's unconscious, and to some extent conscious, knowledge of the existence of the anus which plays a more frequently observed part in infantile sexual theories.

The first introjected object, the mother's breast, forms the basis of the super-ego. Just as the relation to the mother's breast precedes and strongly influences the relation to the father's penis, so the relation to the introjected mother affects in many ways the whole course of the super-ego development. Some of the most important features of the super-ego, whether loving and protective or destructive and devouring, are derived from the early maternal components of the super-ego.

The earliest feelings of guilt in both sexes derive from the oral-sadistic desires to devour the mother, and primarily her breasts (Abraham). It is therefore in infancy that feelings of guilt arise. Guilt does not emerge when the Oedipus complex comes to an end, but is rather one of the factors which from the beginning mould its course and affect its outcome.

I wish now to turn specifically to the boy's development. In my view, castration fear starts in infancy as soon as genital sensations are experienced. The boy's early impulses to castrate his father take the form of wishing to bite off his penis, and correspondingly castration fear is first experienced by the boy as the fear lest his own penis should be bitten off. These early castration fears are to begin with overshadowed by anxieties from many other sources, among which internal danger situations play a prominent part. The closer development approaches to genital primacy, the more castration fear comes to the fore. While I thus fully agree with Freud that *castration fear is the leading anxiety situation in the male,* I cannot agree with his description of it as the *single factor* which determines the repression of the Oedipus complex. Early anxieties from various sources contribute all along to the central part which castration fear comes to play in the climax of the Oedipus situation. Furthermore, the boy experiences grief and sorrow in relation to his father as a loved object, because of his impulses to castrate and murder him. For in his good aspects the father is an indispensable source of strength, a friend and an ideal, to whom the boy looks for protection and guidance and whom he therefore feels impelled to preserve. His feelings of guilt about his aggressive impulses towards his father increase his urge to repress his genital desires. Again and again in the analyses of boys and men I have found that feelings of guilt in relation to the loved father were an integral element of the Oedipus complex and vitally influenced its outcome. The feeling that his mother too is endangered by the son's rivalry with the father, and that the father's death would be an irreparable loss to her, contributes to the strength of the boy's sense of guilt and hence to the repression of his Oedipus desires.

Freud, as we know, arrived at the theoretical conclusion that the father, as well as the mother, is an object of the son's libidinal desires. (Cf. his concept of the inverted Oedipus complex.) Moreover, Freud in some of his writings (among his case histories particularly in the 'Analysis of a Phobia in a Five-Year-Old Boy', 1909) has taken account of the part which love for his father plays in the boy's positive Oedipus conflict. He has, however, not given enough weight to the crucial rôle of these feelings of love, both in the development of the Oedipus conflict and in its passing. In my experience the Oedipal situation loses in power not only because the boy is afraid of the destruction of his genital by a revengeful father, but also because he is driven by feelings of love and guilt to preserve his father as an internal and external figure.

I will now briefly state my conclusions about the girl's Oedipus complex. The phase in which, according to Freud, the girl is exclusively attached to her mother already includes, in my view, desires directed towards her father and covers the early stages of the inverted and positive Oedipus complex. While I therefore consider this phase as a period of fluctuation between desires directed towards mother and father in all libidinal positions, there is no doubt in my mind as to the far-reaching and lasting influence of every facet of the relation to the mother upon the relation to the father.

Penis envy and the castration complex play an essential part in the girl's development. But they are very much reinforced by frustration of her positive Oedipus desires. Though the little girl at one stage assumes that her mother possesses a penis as a male attribute, this concept does not play nearly as important a part in her development as Freud suggests. The unconscious theory that her mother contains the admired and desired penis of the father underlies, in my experience, many of the phenomena which Freud described as the relation of the girl to the phallic mother.

The girl's oral desires for her father's penis mingle with her first genital desires to receive that penis. These genital desires imply the wish to receive children from her father, which is also borne out by the equation 'penis = child'. The feminine desire to internalize the penis and to receive a child from her father invariably precedes the wish to possess a penis of her own.

While I agree with Freud about the prominence of the fear of loss of love and of the death of the mother among the girl's anxieties, I hold that the fear of having her body attacked and her loved inner objects destroyed essentially contributes to her main anxiety situation.

FINAL REMARKS

Throughout my description of the Oedipus complex I have attempted to show the interdependence of certain major aspects of development. The sexual development of the child is inextricably bound up with his object relations and with all the emotions which from the beginning mould his attitude to mother and father. Anxiety, guilt and depressive feelings are intrinsic elements of the child's emotional life and therefore permeate the child's early object relations, which consist of the relation to actual people as well as to their representatives in his inner world. From these introjected figures—the child's identifications—the super-ego develops and in turn influences the relation to both parents and the whole sexual development. Thus emotional and sexual development, object relations and super-ego development interact from the beginning.

The infant's emotional life, the early defences built up under the stress of the conflict between love, hatred and guilt, and the vicissitudes of the child's identifications—all these are topics which may well occupy analytic research for a long time to come. Further work in these directions should lead us to a fuller understanding of the personality, which implies a fuller understanding of the Oedipus complex and of sexual development as a whole.

REFERENCES

Freud, S. (1909). Analysis of a phobia in a five-year-old boy. *S.E. 10*, pp. 3–149.

Klein, M. (1932). *The Psychoanalysis of Children*. [Reprinted in *The Writings of Melanie Klein, 2*. London: Hogarth Press, 1975.]

——— (1975). *The Writings of Melanie Klein, 1*. London: Hogarth Press.

O'Shaughnessy, E. (1975). Explanatory Notes. In M. Klein, *The Writings of Melanie Klein, 1* (pp. 436–438). London: Hogarth Press, 1975.

CHAPTER TWO

The missing link: parental sexuality in the Oedipus complex

Ronald Britton

F or Freud the Oedipus complex was the nuclear complex from its discovery in 1897 to the end of his life (Freud, 1897, 1924d). It remained central in the development of the individual for Melanie Klein. She adopted the term 'oedipal situation' and included in it what Freud had referred to as the primal scene, i.e. the sexual relations of the parents both as perceived and as imagined (Klein, 1928; also chapter one, this volume).

From the outset of her work with children Melanie Klein was impressed at the ubiquity of the oedipal situation and its unique importance; she also thought that it began much earlier than did Freud and that it began in relation to part objects before evolving into the familiar Oedipus complex, which related to the two parents perceived as whole objects—that is, as persons. So for her it began in infancy with phantasies of a relation to breast and penis and phantasies of the relationship between these two part

83

objects, which would be succeeded by ideas about the parents under the influence of these earlier phantasies. She felt that the child's attitude and relationship to this unfolding situation was of profound significance for the urge to learn, which she called the epistemophilic impulse, and for the individual's relationship to reality.

In 1926 she wrote,

> at a very early age children become acquainted with reality through the deprivations it imposes on them. They defend themselves against reality by repudiating it. The fundamental thing, however, and the criterion of all later capacity for adaptation to reality is the degree in which they are able to tolerate the deprivations that result from the oedipal situation. [Klein, 1926]

This was written more than a decade before Mrs. Klein was to describe what she called the 'depressive position'— that period of integration and recognition which entailed a realization of the nature of the world outside the self and of the nature of the internal ambivalent feelings towards it, in other words, the beginnings of a sense of external and internal reality and the relationship between them. Since the delineation of this central concept of Kleinian thinking, it has become increasingly evident that the capacity to comprehend and relate to reality is contingent on working through the depressive position. Klein repeatedly emphasized that the Oedipus complex develops hand-in-hand with the developments that make up the depressive position, and I have suggested elsewhere that the working-through of one entails the working through of the other (Britton, 1985).

The initial recognition of the parental sexual relationship involves relinquishing the idea of sole and permanent possession of mother and leads to a profound sense of loss which, if not tolerated, may become a sense of persecution. Later, the oedipal encounter also involves recognition of the difference between the relationship between parents as distinct from the relationship between parent and child: the parents' relationship is genital and procreative; the parent–child relationship is not. This recognition produces a sense of loss and envy, which, if not tolerated, may become a sense of grievance or self-denigration.

The Oedipus situation dawns with the child's recognition of the parents' relationship in whatever primitive or partial form. It is continued by the child's rivalry with one parent for the other, and it is resolved by the child relinquishing his sexual claim on his parents by his acceptance of the reality of their sexual relationship.

In this chapter I want to suggest that if the encounter with the parental relationship starts to take place at a time when the individual has not established a securely based maternal object, the Oedipus situation appears in analysis only in primitive form and is not immediately recognizable as the classical Oedipus complex. In the first part of the chapter I describe a patient who illustrates this situation.

In less severe disorders it is the final relinquishment of the oedipal objects that is evaded. An illusional oedipal configuration is formed as a defensive organization in order to deny the psychic reality of the parental relationship. I emphasize that it is a defence against psychic reality because these defensive phantasies are organized to prevent the emergence of facts already known and phantasies already existent. The parental relationship has been registered but is now denied and defended against by what I call an oedipal illusion. These illusional systems provide what Freud called a

> domain ... separated from the real external world at the time of the introduction of the reality principle ... free from the demand of the exigencies of life, like a kind of reservation. [Freud, 1924e]

In the same passage, he describes the person who creates such a domain in his mind as

lending a special importance and secret meaning to a piece of reality which is different from the reality which is defended against. [ibid.]

In the second part of this chapter I discuss patients who exemplify such oedipal illusions.

In contrast to the fixity of these oedipal illusions, the oedipal rivalry both in the positive (heterosexual) form and in the negative (homosexual) form provides a means of working through the depressive position. In each version one parent is the object of desire, and the other is the hated rival. This configuration is retained, but the feeling changes in relation to each parent. Thus good becomes bad and vice-versa as positive changes to negative. My contention is that the evasive use of this switch is halted by the full recognition of the parents' sexual relationship, their different anatomy, and the child's own nature. This involves the realization that the same parent who is the object of oedipal desire in one version is the hated rival in the other.

The acknowledgement by the child of the parents' relationship with each other unites his psychic world, limiting it to one world shared with his two parents in which different object relationships can exist. The closure of the oedipal triangle by the recognition of the link joining the parents provides a limiting boundary for the internal world. It creates what I call a 'triangular space'—i.e., a space bounded by the three persons of the oedipal situation and all their potential relationships. It includes, therefore, the possibility of being a participant in a relationship and observed by a third person as well as being an observer of a relationship between two people.

To clarify this point it is helpful to remember that observed and imagined events take place in a world conceived of as continuous in space and time (Rey, 1979) and given structure by the oedipal configuration. The capacity to envisage a benign parental relationship influences the development of a space outside the self capable of being observed and thought about, which provides the basis for a belief in a secure and stable world.

The primal family triangle provides the child with two links connecting him separately with each parent and confronts him with the link between them which excludes him. Initially this parental link is conceived in primitive part-object terms and in the modes of his own oral, anal and genital desires, and in terms of his hatred expressed in oral, anal and genital terms. If the link between the parents perceived in love and hate can be tolerated in the child's mind, it provides him with a prototype for an object relationship of a third kind in which he is a witness and not a participant. A third position then comes into existence from which object relationships can be observed. Given this, we can also envisage *being* observed. This provides us with a capacity for seeing ourselves in interaction with others and for entertaining another point of view whilst retaining our own, for reflecting on ourselves whilst being ourselves. This is a capacity we hope to find in ourselves and in our patients in analysis. Anyone, however, who has treated a psychotic patient or been involved in a psychotic transference will know what I mean when I refer to times when this seems impossible, and it is at those times that one realizes what it means to lack that third position.

A patient who exemplifies difficulties in the first encounters with the oedipal situation

In my early work with this patient, Miss A, I was hardly aware that my difficulties in understanding her had anything to do with the Oedipus complex. What gradually became evident was that she lacked the 'third position' described above. She could not conceive of relationships between others, and it was intolerable for her to feel that I was communing with myself about her.

Miss A came into treatment after a psychotic breakdown in midlife. She was relatively soon afterwards able to carry on an ostensibly normal life in the outside world, but she remained for many years in a psychotic state of mind in her sessions and in relation to me.

I came to learn that she could not allow the notion of parental intercourse to exist because she could only anticipate it as a disaster. The possibility of my communicating with a third object was unthinkable for her, and so the third position I refer to was untenable.

As a consequence it seemed impossible to disentangle myself sufficiently from the to-and-fro of the interaction to know what was going on. In the early years of her analysis I found that any move of mine towards that which by another person would have been called objectivity could not be tolerated. We were to move along a single line and meet at a single point. There was to be no lateral movement. A sense of space could be achieved only by increasing the distance between us, a process she found hard to bear unless she initiated it. What I felt I needed desperately was a place in my mind that I could step into sideways from which I could look at things. If I tried to force myself into such a position by asserting a description of her in analytic terms, she would become violent, sometimes physically, sometimes by screaming. When it became a little more contained, she could express it in words: she shouted: 'Stop that fucking thinking!' I came to realize that these efforts of mine to consult my analytic self were detected by her and experienced as a form of internal intercourse of mine, which corresponded to parental intercourse. This she felt threatened her existence. If I turned to something in my mind later on, when things were not so primitive, she felt I was eliminating my experience of her in my mind. The only way I found of finding a place to think that was helpful and not disruptive was to allow the evolution within myself of my own experience and *to articulate this to myself,* whilst communicating to her *my understanding of her point of view.* This, I found, did enlarge the possibilities, and my patient could begin to think. It seemed to me that it was a model in which parental intercourse could take place if the knowledge of it did not force itself in some intrusive way into the child's mind. Should it do so, it appeared to be felt to be annihilating the child's link with her mother both externally and internally.

In an attempt to understand this clinical situation, I have called on Bion's concept of the 'container and contained', in addition to Melanie Klein's theories of the early Oedipus situation. Bion (1959) has described the consequences for some individuals of a failure of maternal containment as the development within them of a destructive envious superego that prevents them from learning or pursuing profitable relations with any object. He makes it clear that the inability of the mother to take in her child's projections is experienced *by the child* as a destructive attack *by her* on his link and communication *with her* as his good object.

The idea of a good maternal object can only be regained by splitting off her impermeability so that now a hostile force is felt to exist, which attacks his good link with his mother. Mother's goodness is now precarious and depends on him restricting his knowledge of her. Enlargement of knowledge of her as a consequence of development and his curiosity are felt to menace this crucial relationship. Curiosity also discloses the existence of the oedipal situation. This in the development of every child is a challenge to his belief in the goodness of his mother, and a reluctance to admit it into his picture of his mother is normal. In the child already menaced by any enlargement of his knowledge of his mother because of her existing precarious status in his mind, the further threat of acknowledging her relationship with father is felt to spell disaster. The rage and hostility that would be aroused by this discovery is felt to threaten his belief in a world where good objects can exist. The hostile force that was thought to attack his original link with his mother is now equated with the oedipal father, and the link between the parents is felt to reconstitute her as the non-receptive deadly mother. The child's original link with the good maternal object is felt to be the source of life, and so, when it is threatened, life is felt to be threatened.

In some personalities, therefore, the full recognition of parental sexuality is felt as a danger to life. The emergence in the transference of the full emotional significance for them of an idea of the primal scene is followed by panic attacks and fear of imminent death. Greater knowledge of the oedipal situation is also felt to initiate a mental catastrophe.

Faced with this—as Klein (1946) and Bion (1956) have pointed out—the psychotic mutilates his mind in order not to perceive it. In schizophrenic patients the mental appar- atus is splintered, and thinking becomes impossible. The patient I am describing, Miss A, appeared to have preserved a great deal by a violent severance of her mind so that some parts were protected from knowledge and only emerged in a psychotic breakdown or in analysis.

There was in her an 'infantile' self that appeared ignorant of anything other than an ideal breast and a state of persecution. The persecutor was a hovering male presence, which she feared might oust the good mother, and she was terrified she might be left alone with this figure. Interruptions in analysis and any interruptions in the flow of good experience were felt to be the result of violent attacks from this hostile object. At times I was taken to be this hostile object; at other times I was felt to be the victim

of it. I was also familiar with it in the form of my patient
attacking me. As progress was made and communications
between us became more possible, her internal situation
became clearer. She contained a hostile object, or part of
herself in fusion with a hostile object, that interfered in her
attempts to communicate with me. At times this had the
power to control her speech, and she could not articulate. At
others she whispered words, and broken phrases were
managed. If I could demonstrate that I really wished to
know her, which I could only do by demonstrating some
minimal understanding, her capacity to communicate
would be recovered. The way I came to understand that
often-repeated sequence was that she needed some experience of my taking her in *before* I could return in her mind as
the good maternal object she could talk to. Otherwise I
might be what she called the 'wrong person'.

The 'wrong person' looked like the right person but had
connections with father. For many years she was
threatened by the fear of these crucially distinguished
figures becoming confused. The thought of her idealized
mother becoming united with father was her greatest fear.
In the transference it took the form of a fear that the
different aspects of my relationship with her would not be
distinct from each other. Some of my functions were
regarded as good; others as bad, such as my going away; She
kept them distinct in her mind as if they were different
transference figures. 'Don't become one thing,' she would
say at times, in terror. From this patient I learnt how
essential it was to distinguish between the integration that
is sought for as a means of working through the depressive
position, and a fusion of elements that are not stabilized and
distinguished in their qualities and attributes, and whose
union produces a sense of chaos.

If any pressure towards precocious integration was felt to
come from me, it provoked great anxiety and either violent
refusal or abject masochistic submission. This latter reac-

tion turned out to be based on a phantasy of submission to a sadistic father and was regarded by my patient as profoundly wicked but always tempting. It appeared to serve the purpose of substituting herself for mother; such substitution provided both perverse gratification and an avoidance of the phantasy of the parents uniting.

She felt I must not become 'one thing'—i.e. a monstrous amalgamation of the separate maternal and paternal identities she had attributed to me. The amalgam that would result from this union was an ostensibly loving maternal figure who had inside her a contradiction of her own nature; a presence that made all her apparent good qualities treacherous. I was always reminded of descriptions of demonic possession, in which the devil was felt to have infused all the characteristics of the person with hidden evil. The horror she felt about this figure was to do with its contradictory nature. She called it 'unnatural' and regarded the emergence of this idea of me in the transference as disastrous because it destroyed not only all good but also all meaning previously established.

This fearful outcome corresponds to Melanie Klein's description of the child's terror of the combined object as a persecutory phantasy of the parents fused in permanent intercourse. I would describe my patient as having an infantile phantasy that her father was of such a nature and power that he could penetrate her mother's identity in such a way as to corrupt her goodness, and maternal goodness, although precariously idealized, was my patient's only concept of goodness. It always impressed me that for such a patient the very concept of goodness was at stake and not simply its availability or presence.

It is not my intention here to go into the factors in the patient's disposition and life circumstances that contributed to this inability to surmount the earliest stages of the Oedipus situation in any detail. I would simply like to say that in my view it was the initial failure of maternal containment that made the negotiation of the Oedipus complex impossible. The personality and intrusiveness of her father into her mother's mind were very significant, but these were combined with the patient's own considerable difficulty in tolerating frustration. The phantasy of parental intercourse was constructed from a combination of projections of herself and perceptions of her parents.

My wish is to draw attention to the reality of her belief that catastrophe was associated with the emergence of the oedipal situation and that consequently she resorted to violent splitting to prevent it occurring. The result was an internal division within her mind organized around separate parental objects whose conjunction she believed must be prevented.

External reality may provide an opportunity for benign modification of such phantasies, or it may lend substance to fears. It may also provide material for the formation of psychic structures that are meant to prevent the recognition of the Oedipus situation. The situation in the family of my patient enabled her to construct an internal organization of herself and her objects which had three main parts with no integration of them.

Her everyday relationship with the outside world, which was superficial, undemanding and reasonable, was based on her relationship with her sibling. Internally she had one self in loving union with an idealized mother and another self in alliance with a father seen as epitomizing anti-mother love. The link between these two selves was missing, as was the link between the internal parents.

What these two 'selves' did have in common, when it eventually emerged, was hatred of the parents as a loving couple. Initially the two parents could only be perceived as being linked in hate and mutual incompatibility, which meant that their coming together was a disaster. The gradual reclaiming by the patient of projected parts of herself in the course of a long and very difficult treatment led to the emergence of the idea of a couple who could unite willingly and pleasurably. New difficulties then arose with the eruption of envy and jealousy; these emotions were felt to be unbearable and seemed to become almost pure psychic pain.

I would like to distinguish the problems of this patient from the others referred to in this chapter whose difficulties with the Oedipus situation were not so early, total or primitive. The difference clinically could be summarized by saying that in this patient they were in the manner and mode of the paranoid–schizoid position. I think aetiologically the difference lay in the failure to establish a securely based good maternal object before encountering the vicissitudes of the Oedipus complex.

Oedipal illusions

As described briefly above, oedipal illusions are a developmentally later phenomenon than the primitive wiping out of the parental relationship with delusional developments that I have described in the previous section. When these illusions are paramount, the parental relationship is known but its full significance is evaded and its nature, which demonstrates the differences between the parental relationship and the parent–child relationship, is not acknowledged.

The illusion is felt to protect the individual from the psychic reality of their phantasies of the oedipal situation. These I have found, in such cases, to be expectations of an endlessly humiliating exposure to parental triumphalism or a disastrous version of parental intercourse. This latter is perceived either as horrific, sado-masochistic or murderous intercourse, or as depressive images of a ruined couple in a ruined world. However, whilst such illusions are perpetuated as evasions of the underlying situation, the Oedipus complex cannot be resolved through the normal processes of rivalry and relinquishment.

I think that in normal development such illusions are frequent and transitory, producing cycles of illusionment and disillusionment that are the familiar features of an analysis. In some people, however, the persistence of an organized oedipal illusion prevents the resolution of the complex and in analysis the full development of its transference counterpart.

These illusions are often conscious—or almost conscious—versions of actual life situations. For example, I heard about a young woman in supervision: she was a musician who gave to her professional relationship with her music teacher the secret significance of preparation for a love affair. Once she was in analysis, her ideas about her analyst were suffused with the same erotic significance and the belief that it would end in marriage.

These wish-fulfilling ideas are often undisclosed in analysis, where they take the form of the patient's belief in a secret understanding between patient and analyst that transcends that formally acknowledged, as Freud points out in his paper 'Observations on transference-love' (Freud, 1915a). The illusory special relationship may take much less conspicuously sexual forms than the example I have quoted, whilst still having an erotized basis.

The transference illusion is felt to protect the patient from what is imagined to be a calamitous transference situation. As such, it poses considerable technical problems. Whilst it persists, all the analyst's communications are interpreted by the patient in the light of the illusional context.

I would like to illustrate the fears defended against by such an illusional construction from the analysis of a male patient. He had originally been a refugee from a foreign country but now worked as a government scientist. He regarded his parents as having lived separate lives, although they shared the same house. It became clear that the reality of their relationship had given some substance to this idea but also that his fixed mental picture was a caricature. It served as the structure for phantasies involving each parent separately, phantasies that were never integrated, and, though mutually contradictory, they remained adjacent to each other, as it were in parallel.

He transferred his picture to the analytic context in a rigidly literal way. He had a slight acquaintance with my wife in his professional context but never brought any thoughts from that context to his ideas of me as his analyst. He developed pictures in his mind of his analyst and of his analyst's wife in entirely separated contexts. Two wishful outcomes of his analysis lay side by side. One was of a permanent partnership with me in which he and I were alone together; the other was my death coinciding with the end of analysis, when he would marry my widow.

This formed the basis of a complex psychic organization in which the patient was able to oscillate between such contradictory beliefs without ever giving them much reality, or ever giving them up. Whilst this mode was operating in the analysis, things were always about to happen but never did; emotional experiences were about to occur but never materialized. The consequence for the patient's own mental operations was profound. Despite his considerable intellectual gifts, he was not able to bring things together in his mind, which resulted in learning difficulties as a child and a lack of clarity in his thinking as an adult, which had limited his originality. The consequences for his emotional life were a pervasive sense of unreality and a constant feeling of unfulfilment. There was a quality of nonconsummation in all his relationships and projects in life.

When change did begin to occur in his analysis, it provoked phantasies of great violence. Initially they were confined to the night-time. They took the form of murderous intercourse between the primal couple, which filled his dreams in many forms, and when they could not be contained within his dreams, they erupted as transitory night-time hallucinations of a couple who were killing each other.

In contrast to this, the analysis was for a long time an ocean of calm. Calmness was his aim, not fulfilment, and calm detachment was idealized. For a long time this was thought by him to be the aim of analysis and the aspiration of his analyst. Thus he thought his task was to facilitate this in both of us by forever finding agreement. His dreams were enormously informative but were a vehicle for getting rid of his thoughts into me, so that he could relate to my interpretations instead of to them, and therefore to himself second-hand. What his dreams made clear to me was his belief that bringing his parental objects together in his mind would result in explosion and disintegration. When the relationship between us did begin to feel rather different in the sessions, so that we both made more contact and yet were at greater variance, it led to fears of imminent catastrophe.

One form this took was a fear of sudden death. In particular, he had attacks of panic when he thought his heart was about to stop beating. His fearful expectation of violent collision took a concrete form in the emergence of a new fear of driving. Prior to this I had been hearing a lot about 'contra-flow systems' in his sessions—both in dreams and in reports of daily life. (At that time, some years ago, contra-flow traffic systems were a novelty on our motorways and in the news.) I took them to be a representation of the way my patient had segregated so carefully two different and contradictory streams of thought. I had wondered if their appearance in the analysis indicated that things were coming closer together in his mind. My patient then developed a panicky conviction when driving that unless there was a central barrier on the road, the streams of traffic would crash into each other. It reached such proportions that for a time it stopped him driving. This heralded changes in the transference relationship, which now did develop within it some conflict and opposition. The fear of finding within himself the violence that previously had only appeared in projected forms as violent parental intercourse became prominent for the first time. It is best conveyed by a dream he brought after a weekend break, at a time when weekends were very difficult and full of anxiety:

He is about to be left alone in a room with a dangerous, wild man by a couple who are going to the theatre. This man has always been locked up and restrained—he should be in a straitjacket. The patient is terrified that the man would destroy everything in the room. On his own he will not be able to reason with him. The man begins to speak. Previously, it seemed, he had been a mute. Help comes in the form of a Senior Negotiator from the Ministry (where the patient worked in reality). The Negotiator can speak to the Man, but if the Man realizes that the Negotiator has connections with the law, this will provoke him to even greater fury. (In reality, the negotiator was concerned with terrorists in prison.)

The patient had many associations to this dream, and they made it clear that there was a situation in the patient's life involving a sense of betrayal by a woman and sexual jealousy that was connected to the dream. They also made clear that the couple went to the 'Theatre of the Absurd'. This, in turn, was associated with a debate he had participated in once as to whether a theatrical performance in a church could include the word 'fuck'. It was clear, I thought, that the man who represented that aspect of himself that had been mute and locked up was wild with jealousy. That was the new element, in my patient, in his analysis. The debate as to whether the idea of a 'fucking couple' could be allowed in the 'church' of the transference was still taking place in his analysis. My patient's dream suggested that he thought it an 'absurdly' dangerous venture to admit into his mind phantasies of his analyst, as one of a sexual couple, provoking a violent emotional reaction inside him. I interpreted myself as represented by the Negotiator as well as by the parental couple. The law that would further inflame the wild man was, I think, the law of the Oedipus complex—the law that distinguishes the sexes and the generations, provoking not only jealousy but also envy of the parental couple for their sexual and procreative capacities. My intention in describing briefly some aspects of the analysis of this patient is to illustrate some of the fears and conflicts from which the oedipal illusion was felt to protect the patient.

Summary

The oedipal situation begins with the child's recognition of the parents' relationship. In severe disorders development founders at this point, and the Oedipus complex does not appear in recognizable classical form in analysis. The failure to internalize a recognizable oedipal triangle results in a failure to integrate observation and experience. This was the case in the first patient I described. I suggest that it is a consequence of a prior failure of maternal containment.

In the second part of the chapter I described what I call oedipal illusions as defensive phantasies against the psychic reality of the Oedipus situation, and suggested that if they persist, they prevent the normal 'working through' of the Oedipus complex, which is done through sequences of rivalry and relinquishment.

Finally, I would like to clarify my view of the normal development of the Oedipus complex. It begins with the child's recognition of the nature of the parental relationship and the child's phantasies about it. In the Oedipus myth this would be represented by the story of the infant Oedipus abandoned on the hillside by his mother—a tragic version in the child's phantasy of being left to die whilst the parents sleep together. The complex unfolds further in the development of the child's rivalry with one parent for absolute possession of the other. This we see exemplified in the myth by the meeting at the crossroads where Laius bars the way, as if representing the father's obstruction of the child's wish to re-enter mother through her genital. This is what I regard as the psychic reality of the Oedipus complex, as are the fears of personal or parental death as imagined consequences.

What I have called oedipal illusions are defensive phantasies meant to occlude these psychic realities. In the myth I see the oedipal illusion as the state in which Oedipus is on the throne with his wife/mother, surrounded by his court, turning a 'blind eye', as John Steiner has put it, as to what they already half know but choose to ignore (Steiner, 1985). In this situation, where illusion reigns supreme, curiosity is felt to spell disaster. In the phantasied tragic version of the Oedipus complex the discovery of the oedipal triangle is felt to be the death of the couple: the nursing couple or the parental couple. In this phantasy the arrival of the notion of a third always murders the dyadic relationship.

I think this idea is entertained by all of us at some time; for some it appears to remain a conviction, and when it does it leads to serious psychopathology. I have suggested that it is through mourning for this lost exclusive relationship that it can be realized that the oedipal triangle does not spell the death of a relationship, but only the death of an idea of a relationship.

REFERENCES

Bion, W. R. (1956). Development of schizophrenic thought. *Int. J. Psycho-Anal.*, *37*, 344–346. [Reprinted in *Second Thoughts.* London: Heinemann, 1967.]

_____ (1959). Attacks on linking. *Int. J. Psycho-Anal.*, *40*, 308–315. [Reprinted in *Second Thoughts* (pp. 93–109). London: Heinemann, 1967.]

Britton, R. S. (1985). The Oedipus complex and the depressive position. *Sigmund Freud House Bulletin, Vienna, 9,* 7–12.

Freud, S. (1897). Letter 71. Extracts from the Fliess Papers. *S.E. 1* (pp. 263–266).

_____ (1915a). Observations on transference-love. *S.E. 12* (pp. 157–171).

_____ (1924d). The dissolution of the Oedipus complex. *S.E. 19* (pp. 171–179).

_____ (1924e). The loss of reality in neurosis and psychosis. *S.E. 19* (pp. 183–187).

Klein, M. (1926). The psychological principles of early analysis. *Int. J. Psycho-Anal.*, *7.* [Reprinted in *The Writings of Melanie Klein, 1* (pp. 128–138). London: Hogarth Press, 1975.]

_____ (1928). Early stages of the Oedipus conflict. *Int. J. Psycho-Anal., 9,* 167–180. [Reprinted in *The Writings of Melanie Klein, 1* (pp. 186–198). London: Hogarth Press, 1975.]

_____ (1946). Notes on some schizoid mechanisms. *Int. J. Psycho-Anal., 27,* 99–110. [Reprinted in *The Writings of Melanie Klein, 3* (pp. 1–24). London: Hogarth Press, 1975.]

Rey, J. H. (1979). Schizoid phenomena in the borderline. In J. LeBoit & A.Capponi (Eds.), *Advances in the Psychotherapy of the Borderline Patient* (pp. 449–484). New York: Jason Aronson.

Steiner, J. (1985). Turning a blind eye: The cover up for Oedipus. *Int. Rev. Psychoanal., 12,* 161–172.

CHAPTER THREE

The Oedipus complex: manifestations in the inner world and the therapeutic situation

Michael Feldman

Melanie Klein expanded our understanding of the Oedipus complex by developing the notion of the child's internal world, inhabited by figures derived from early experiences, whose qualities and functions are influenced by projections and distortions. She showed how, in the child's phantasy, these figures relate to one another in complex ways, and some of these relationships constitute early versions of the Oedipus complex (Klein, 1928, 1932; also chapter one in this volume). Part of the power of her clinical theories derives from the way she was able to use her understanding of the nature and relationships of these internal figures to recognize what was being experienced and enacted by the child, in the clinical situation, as it was made manifest in the transference.

I would like to use three clinical fragments to illustrate some points that derive from this. First, the familiar but compelling phenomenon of the way in which the patient's experience of the figures of his childhood remains alive in his mind and influences his current relationships, including

103

the way he experiences and uses the analyst. One of the characteristics of the oedipal situation, which is reflected in the analysis, is that the participants often find themselves faced with a difficult 'moral' dilemma, rather than a clear choice. Each finds himself pulled in more than one direction, and each option seems to involve a compromise and may require a blurring or avoidance of aspects of reality that arouse too much pain or guilt. Needless to say, in the original story Oedipus did not make a conscious decision to kill his father and marry his mother; the choices that presented themselves to all the participants seemed to be the best ones at the time, and the marriage had the approbation of the people of Thebes, even though there were those who knew the truth and presumably considered it best to remain silent. The awful reality emerged only slowly, with difficulty, and at considerable cost (Steiner, 1985).

I hope to illustrate not only the way in which these subtle dilemmas are conveyed in the analytic material, but how the analyst often finds himself drawn into a re-enactment of the dilemma that was originally the child's, but in which the parent has become inescapably involved. The development of our understanding of the processes of projective and introjective identification, which we owe to Mrs. Klein and a number of research workers who followed, makes it clear that some of these complexities are inevitable. There is often a partial and shifting identification with each parent, and each parent becomes, in turn, imbued with qualities projected into him or her by the child. The drama thus often involves complex reversals, and the analyst's role vis-à-vis these different figures must reflect some of these complexities.

It is only by careful attention to the dynamics of the session, in particular to the countertransference experience (including the subtle pressure on the analyst to act in particular ways), that some of these aspects of the Oedipus situation can be recognized. They are often derived from a very early period of the patient's experience and were not represented in his mind in words, but in feelings or actions or impulses towards action. Even if they do derive from slightly later stages of development, they often involve perceptions and interactions with parental figures that were characterized not by verbalization, but by uneasy collusions or evasions. I hope to show how this gives rise not simply to problems in understanding the patient, his fantasies, anxieties and conflicts, but to technical difficulties for the analyst in knowing how to handle the situation and deal with the pressures that draw him into an enactment of aspects of the oedipal situation.

While it is the *child* who has to cope with conflicting wishes in the context of the family relationships, he may use projective mechanisms to rid himself of such conflict, which then become the parent's responsibility. The parent may then find himself in a dilemma, which results partly from his own oedipal conflicts and partly from those projected into him by the child. Because of his or her conscious or unconscious awareness of the intensity of the emotions involved, any course of action has important implications. To take a simple example: if a father is made aware of his young daughter's intense sexual and aggressive impulses (perhaps through a partial identification with an excluded child) and then has some inkling of the nature of the phantasies in which both he and the mother are involved, then taking his daughter on his knee may further stimulate her belief in their excited sexual alliance against the mother. Not to take her on his knee may be to reject her, perhaps giving evidence of his unease about the situation, and thus confirming, in a different way, the child's oedipal phantasies.

There is thus no way the father can behave that will not stimulate the child's aggressive and/or sexual phantasies.

What the child needs of him is some awareness of these impulses, with a sufficiently firm base within himself (part of which involves experiencing himself as a member of a mature couple), so that the child's impulses and phantasies (and his own) have neither to be denied, nor acted out.

This underlying model is both re-experienced and re-created in the analytic situation and will of course determine the nature and quality of the transference and countertransference. What I want to illustrate in the clinical material that follows is how the patient's material and the dynamics of the transference situation can lead us to understand the individual's experience and allow us to construct a view of the nature of the parental interaction, and the way the patient relates to it.

One important consequence of this view of the oedipal configurations that exist in the patient's inner world is that it enables us to study their influence on his basic mental functions. If the patient negotiates the Oedipus complex in a relatively healthy way, he has an internal model of an intercourse that is, on balance, a creative activity. This seems to be directly connected with the development of the patient's capacity to allow thoughts and ideas to interact in a kind of healthy intercourse. On the other hand, the phantasy that any connection forms a bizarre or predominantly destructive couple seems to result in damaged, perverse or severely inhibited forms of thinking. In my clinical examples I try to examine the nature of the oedipal couple existing in the patient's mind, partly derived from his perceptions and partly distorted by projection. This not only influences the patient's experience of the transference but also tends to manifest itself by engaging the analyst in a re-enactment of the oedipal conflicts. Finally, I hope to indicate some of the ways in which the patient's phantasies regarding the nature of these relationships influence his thinking.

The first case concerns a young man whom I treated some years ago; the analysis ended when the patient had to go abroad, but I had been able to keep detailed notes, and many aspects of the case remain fresh in my mind. He was the youngest of four sons, and his parents were both involved in the theatre. His mother was, at that time, a talented and successful actress.

He began a session following a long weekend in silence; he then began to speak in a constricted, self-conscious, quite frustrating way. He made no mention of the weekend but referred after a while to a dream he had had. In the dream, he was on a stage, parading himself, dressed in silk underclothes similar to the ones he recalled his mother wearing as she prepared herself for the theatre. There were not many people in the audience, but he particularly noticed an older man, who looked rather dishevelled and who seemed to be tantalized and excited by him. The man was, however, forced to remain on the other side of the footlights, as if separated from him by a pane of glass. The patient said he thought this man was a 'pure homosexual'. He had linked the figure to myself, and this had been a source of pleasure and excitement. He also seemed to be quite excited while telling me about the dream.

The patient had always felt himself deprived of proper attention and love. While his parents presented themselves as sympathetic and caring (and in many ways did their best, I think), the patient never felt properly looked after and never fully believed in the quality of their care, or that he could ever properly hold the attention of either parent. He tried to overcome this by offering himself to them as 'special'—either he was especially ill or unhappy, especially good, or, sometimes, especially exciting to one or other parent.

With his father in particular, there seems to have been the phantasy of taking the mother's place, and this seemed to have been expressed on the weekend by the dream in which he made himself exciting by getting into her clothes. And yet, in a sad and touching way, he conveyed that he never really believed that any of this would succeed. In his dream the man was a 'pure homosexual', which meant someone who had no interest in real women, but who found my patient, dressed in women's underclothes, tantalizing and exciting. The dream demonstrated the absence of any proper contact between my patient (who was identified with a peculiar, contrived figure) and the man for whom he was parading himself in this theatrical fashion. On the contrary, it makes explicit his sense of being cut off from his objects, as if by a pane of glass.

This corresponded very closely to the patient's experience in the past, when he felt doubtful about being able to engage his parents' attention properly, whatever he did, and his experience in the analysis, where he often felt he had to produce something that would really grip my attention. At times he seemed to believe, or at least half-believe, that he could succeed, but at other times he had to produce more and more bizarre actions, which might even then not have the desired effect.

I thought the patient had dealt with the experience of the long weekend, my absence, and his feelings of loneliness, jealousy and frustration by projecting, in his phantasy, the feeling of being left out, excited and tantalized. By reversing the roles, he replaced me and became a figure who paraded himself in this provocative way. Moreover, this was not simply a phantasy that relieved him during the weekend, but one that was partially enacted during the session. The patient's initial silence, his hesitant and provocative way of speaking, and the sense of being in possession of exciting and provocative mental underwear— his dreams or sexual fantasies, which I would be interested in—made this real in the session. He always tried very hard to judge what would interest me, and what would affect me, and hence make him special for me. He was touchingly preoccupied with the need to be the patient who I was most interested in or excited by, or the patient who understood me best, was most sensitive to my state of health, or my state of mind. At other times, he seemed to want to be the patient who unsettled me the most, who caused me the most concern, the one with whom I would remain preoccupied between sessions.

However, as I have indicated, this often failed in its desired effect, and rather than evoking curiosity, jealousy or excitement, he was more likely to provoke feelings of sympathy, concern or at times even despair.

There are various ways of understanding the nature of the countertransference experience with this patient. It often seemed that when he was in possession of intense and disturbing feelings he was not properly able to employ projective mechanisms to reach his object. Thus, some of the problems in his early relationship with his parents might derive from the fact that his failure to communicate with them properly by means of projective identification made it difficult for them actually to know what was going on in him, as they did not properly feel the impact of his needs and his anxieties.

The other aspect of this concerns the way in which his objects were perceived and experienced. Bion (1959) described the situation in which the infant is confronted with a parental figure who responds dutifully to him without being able to receive or tolerate the infant's projections, which then become more and more violent and disordered, giving rise to a hopeless, vicious circle.

My experience in the transference convinced me that there was very little conception of a parental object capable of containing what he might project into it, or of a healthy oedipal couple, engaged in a creative intercourse—which implies, of course, the relation of container and contained. Instead, there was a couple who went through the motions of being linked, while actually separated by the footlights or by a pane of glass.

This could be the product of his envious attack on such a couple, which as a consequence presented itself to his mind as a bizarre, combined parental object, such as that described by Melanie Klein (1932). Alternatively, he might have had a perception or an intuitive sense of the parental couple as being, in fact, damaged—a pathetic, confused combined figure. Although they presented themselves to him as healthy and exciting, as if meaning to evoke his envy and jealousy, they largely failed to do so, and he was actually confronted with a more disturbing situation. He thus re-created in the analysis the oedipal situation in which there was a bizarre figure, composed of elements of mother and father, which was meant to arouse a great deal of excitement and jealousy, but which had a much more awful effect in that it evoked pity and a feeling of hopelessness.

For much of the time, the two of us were felt to constitute such a bizarre, uncreative couple, or he would perceive me as posturing as a healthy, vigorous object, but one that he knew to be peculiar and damaged and hence indistinguishable from himself. There were other times, however, when he seemed able to recognize a difference between us, and this allowed us to do real analytic work for a time, which was accompanied by a sense of relief and gratitude. It was striking that at such times his own thinking acquired a different quality—it was more coherent, and he seemed to have a real sense that things in his world had meaning. At times like this, there was much less vagueness, excitement and fragmentation in the way his mind worked. However, such periods of constructive work were short-lived and stimulated a desperate, destructive envious attack.

As I have indicated, there seemed to be a relationship between the quality of the patient's thinking and the nature of the oedipal couple represented in phantasy and reflected in the transference at any given time. The patient usually found it extremely difficult to make proper connections in his own mind, to do any thinking for himself. Instead, his 'thinking' often consisted of the agglomeration of two ideas in a peculiar way, with no meaningful link between them. As we saw in his dream, he would often present this bizarre conjunction as if it were desirable, even exciting. Just as he found it difficult to tolerate any knowledge of the disturbing quality of the parental relationship (and felt his parents could not tolerate it), so he found it painful and frightening to face what went on in his own mind, and he was driven into making these peculiar, desperate combinations, which were often accompanied by excitement and always by a sense of isolation.

Although I thought he was not properly able to use projective mechanisms to communicate his feelings and anxieties, at times he felt driven to project these more desperate and disordered functions into his object. In the countertransference I experienced them in the form of a pressure to make banal interpretations or to link things in a way that would 'do' but did not feel right, and which I knew to be of no use. The effect of doing this was to relieve both of us temporarily, while increasing an underlying feeling of frustration and despair.

When I was able to resist this pressure to enter into the world of the dream and retain my capacity to think in a different way, even though this was sometimes difficult and painful, it seemed to strengthen the patient's contact with reality and with his own internal world.

I would now like to turn to a second case, that of a young woman in whom the oedipal couple was represented very differently, with a different set of phantasies and anxieties structuring the transference. The patient's thinking was affected by her need constantly to provide internal reassurance against her fears of being rejected or attacked, and there was a corresponding pressure on the analyst to fit in with this.

The patient's parents had separated when she was very young, and her childhood had been dominated by a painful and difficult relationship with her mother, a very disturbed woman. Her mother criticized and denigrated the absent father, blaming him for everything, always putting herself completely in the right. My patient was under considerable pressure to accept this version, and any attempt to question the truth of what was presented to her was liable to produce an angry and violent response. She gradually became aware of the degree of her mother's disturbance and the elaborate web of lies and distortions with which she had grown up, but she was always too frightened to challenge this.

At the same time she entertained secret phantasies of her father returning to rescue her. It was important for her to imagine that he would see that she had done her very best; it was she who had not only done well at school, but had also tidied up the house and cooked the meals. He could hardly fail to take her side and recognize how bad, cruel and neglectful her mother was and take her away with him. The alternative scenario, which she hardly dared contemplate, was that mother and father would 'gang up' against her, identify her as aggressive, nasty and dirty and get rid of her.

In the session prior to the one I will describe in detail, the patient had brought up familiar difficulties in the relationship with her partner, where she often felt painfully rejected. She was quite defensive about her contribution to any of the problems, and it took some time before she was able to acknowledge her own hostility and resentment. As the session proceeded, she became less defensive, and a more complex, real picture of their interaction began to emerge. She seemed to feel something important had been addressed and felt some relief.

She arrived a few minutes late for the next session, and she carefully explained how she had been delayed by things that were quite beyond her control. She then said that something had happened the previous day that she felt tempted to push away, but then thought she ought to talk about it, especially as there was nothing else she could think of to say. She described how busy she had been with a variety of tasks and emphasized how well she had coped. She had been able to remain very patient and calm with all the people she had had to deal with. Her partner had had a meeting to attend in the evening, and as he was very short of time, she had prepared a nice snack for him to eat in her car. She had been very patient and understanding and had raised no objections to his going out, even though she had seen very little of him.

There was a sing-song tone to her voice, and I had a fairly good idea that the story would turn out in a familiar way, with my patient let down, hurt and disappointed.

When her partner returned from his meeting, he was very tired and just sat in front of the television. He said he wanted to hear the news, and she did not mind, although she had heard it herself an hour before. While sitting there, he dozed off, which I knew often irritated her.

Then his friend Peter telephoned, and he spoke to Peter for about half an hour. It was nothing urgent or connected with his work (which she could have understood)—they were just chatting. She suddenly felt absolutely furious—he was too tired to bother with her but had the energy to speak to his friend. It was not that she was making any great demands on him, or anything like that, she just wanted a bit of attention.

This all sounded extremely reasonable and compelling. There was a tone in her voice that pulled me into agreeing completely with her, being unequivocally 'on her side'. I was struck by the extent to which it had been necessary for her to build up a case, as it were, emphasizing how good and tolerant she had been all evening. She made a point of acknowledging that she had been able to deal with the difficulties in this way because of the help she had received in the previous session, and spelled out that she had accepted the idea that her anger and resentment might have an effect on her partner, which was one reason why she had tried to be so good and patient. I tried to take up this need to place herself beyond reproach, and to demarcate so clearly that it was her partner who behaved inconsiderately and unappreciatively. Actually, it was clear that although she referred to the helpful session and the recognition of a more complex interaction between herself and her partner, I thought she had in fact been engaged in repudiating what she perceived as my doubts about her. She would demonstrate to me that her partner treated her in an aggressive or hurtful way, even if her conduct was beyond reproach. There was considerable pressure on me to agree with this point of view, to acknowledge that I was wrong to have any doubts about her and to join her in an unreserved condemnation of her partner. When, instead of simply fitting into this, I pointed out this pressure, what then occurred in the session seemed to be a repetition of the scene on the previous evening. She felt hurt and misunderstood, offended and puzzled by my failure to join her. It was as if I was either siding with her partner against her or was only interested in attending to what *I* was interested in (like her partner talking to Peter on the telephone). Both alternatives made her feel rebuffed and again raised the possibility that I might suspect her of containing, within her, something undesirable.

I have briefly outlined some of the experiences and phantasies that I think preoccupied my patient during her childhood and adolescence. The point I wish to stress is the extent to which she felt driven, like her mother, to maintain a position in which she was in the right and the other person was responsible for all the damage. As with her mother, this often had a frantic, desperate quality about it, as it served to fend off the alternative view, where she herself would be recognized as being full of angry, destructive, jealous and sexual impulses, which were felt to be extremely threatening. For my patient in particular, if she were identified as 'bad', she would be lost: mother would violently attack her, and father would never rescue her—on the contrary, he might form an alliance with mother against her. Her jealous oedipal wishes were not completely split off, however, and she had some awareness of the very impulses that she was at such pains to repudiate. Indeed, part of the motive for being so good was in fact to prevent any possibility of the couple coming together, whether the couple was the original parental couple, myself and her partner forming an alliance that excluded her, or my entertaining my own thoughts, which I might use to do my work. I hope it is evident how much this was enacted in the session I have reported. I thought the patient did have some inkling of the ways in which she subtly attacked and provoked her partner and of her impulse to stop me doing any analytic work with her, even when she appeared to be so appreciative. Her knowledge of this caused her considerable anxiety, however, either because it might lead me to attack (like her mother), or because I might abandon her in favour of a different alliance.

It was not clear how much conflict the *patient* was conscious of, and she certainly had great difficulty in tolerating ambivalence or conflict, but there was no doubt about the *analyst* being placed in a dilemma. On the one hand, there was a pressure to agree with the patient's point of view—it seemed a reasonable, kind and supportive way for a parent (or analyst) to respond, and it contained no evident harm. Moreover, it seemed unsympathetic or hurtful to entertain doubts, to be seen, perhaps, as siding with the partner who had treated her so badly. I had no doubt, however, that the pressure was in part a seductive invitation to collude in a way that supported a phantasy of the two of us forming an intimate couple, to the exclusion of the partner, who would function as a receptacle for all the unwelcome elements.

And yet one has to tolerate the discomfort of the uncertainty that any support or closeness could be erotized and used in this way, otherwise one would be driven to become too suspicious and too distant. The patient's conflict is thus largely projected into the analyst, who is then faced with what seems like a technical problem, but which has its roots in the 'moral' problem of the parent, who in this case seemed to be invited to join in a collusive relationship that excluded conflict and doubt and, indeed, attacked reality.

As with the patient described above, it was possible to follow the way this was being enacted not only in the transference, but also within the patient's own mind. She spent a good deal of time reassuring herself about how good she was being, in the way she did in the session, although this did not completely succeed in fending off her doubts and suspicions, as I had not been totally convinced by the split she presented to me. Although it was clear that she had some knowledge of her own aggression and provocativeness, the prospect of facing the truth was associated with the phantasy of being violently separated from an object she needed and depended on, but which had virtually no capacity for tolerating anything bad.

In this patient, in contrast to the one described previously, her primary objects were, in phantasy, differentiated from one another. There was, moreover, a notion of them coming together in intercourse, although she saw this as very fraught and easily leading to catastrophe if any difficulty should arise. She was much more able to put things together in her own mind, although the nature and extent of her anxiety whenever she had to face some internal difficulty was such that she resorted to a variety of subtle internal as well as external evasions and denials. One of the ways in which she was able to make use of the analysis was at times to internalize a relationship with an object that was able to tolerate this, which brought her immense relief. What is striking is the way her own thinking became more expansive and flexible. She could then allow her own thoughts to link up in a freer, more fluid way, without the fear that this intercourse within her own mind would lead to abandonment. This greatly expanded her capacity for understanding, and as a result the objects that inhabited her world became more 'three-dimensional'.

The third case has some similarities to the one I have just mentioned, although there are a number of important differences. The patient's model of the parental relationship was of a violent, intrusive and potentially disastrous interaction, albeit one full of excitement. My patient demonstrated a variety of techniques for protecting herself against such an interaction, both within the analysis and in her outside life. Any effort I made to reach her was liable to be construed as an intrusive and dangerous threat, which had to be evaded. This configuration existed in her own mind as well, and she often felt the need to avoid making explicit the connections that existed there, to protect herself from anxiety and pain. In the analysis, she was able to solve this problem to a large extent by forcefully projecting the potentially dangerous thoughts and understanding into me; she could then use familiar and effective methods to defend herself against the threat, which was now an *external* one.

The patient had presented for treatment with a number of symptoms, including quite severe sexual difficulties associated with feelings of panic, which accompanied any threat of intimacy. Her symptoms improved a good deal, but the threat of intimate contact which she could not control remained a problem for her. In the analysis, her anxiety expressed itself in her long silences, the caution with which she revealed what was in her mind, and the way she was inclined to fend off interpretations. At the same time she left me in no doubt that she had an active and intelligent mind and was deeply engaged in the analysis, which was very important to her, though rarely acknowledged as such.

Just before the session I wish to describe, the patient had recalled, for the first time, an incident from her childhood— something, as she told me, that she had not witnessed directly but had been told about. When she was five years old and already attending school, a truck carrying a boiler had gone out of control, had crashed through the tall thick hedge in front of their house and come to rest just in front of the living room, where her mother and grandmother were sitting at the time. When she arrived back from school, a crane had already removed the truck. After a pause she said it occurred to her now that if it were not for that thick hedge, the truck might have demolished the house.

This was one example of an image that recurred in the patient's material, reflecting an anxiety that expressed itself in her problems with any form of intimacy. There was an object that intruded in a violent and uncontrolled manner (in this case threatening mother and grandmother). It illustrated the need for a protective barrier—in this case the thick hedge—which just managed to avert a catastrophe. Sometimes she felt I did not understand this and that I tried to encourage her to leave herself more exposed. She often reassured herself that it was, after all, vital to have such protection and conjured up images of what might have happened to her objects (or herself) without it.

The emergence of the material at this particular time reflected the fact that the patient was feeling a little safer and had allowed herself to be more open. She had begun a new sexual relationship and had been able to talk about it in the sessions, but this greater accessibility had been followed by withdrawal into silence and greater resistance.

Shortly after this she arrived for a session ten minutes late and slightly out of breath. She said she was sorry she was late, she had had a number of things to attend to before she left her flat, and she should have left more time. She was then silent. I found myself feeling a bit frustrated and thinking ruefully that after years of analysis she accounted for her lateness in such superficial and un-insightful terms. As she began to speak again, I suddenly recalled something I had forgotten—namely, that this was the day her parents were making a rare visit to this country and were due to stay with my patient in her flat for a few days. Her remark about having a number of things to attend to contained an implicit reference to this, and the fact that they would arrive before she returned from her teaching job.

She was intensely preoccupied with what her parents might learn of her private life—particularly about her sexual life, and also about her analysis (which she treated rather similarly, as far as her parents were concerned). It had never been possible for her to discuss any of her relationships with her parents, and she described the elaborate precautions she intended to take to hide any evidence of her sexuality—such as hiding suspender belts and a frilly nightgown she had received as a present in a locked cupboard, or in the loft above her flat. She was equally secretive about her analysis, and when they visited her and she was unable to account for her absence, she unhesitatingly missed the session. For this visit, she had worked out an elaborate compromise—attending some of the sessions and telling them it was connected with her work, and missing some sessions. I think there is a phantasy that both parents, in different ways, are intensely curious, and rather intrusive, particularly about her sexual life.

These matters could never be openly referred to within the family, although she conveyed that there was a highly charged atmosphere, with each member of the family having suspicions and fantasies about what was going on. This was of course reflected in the analysis, where it proved difficult to find ways of speaking about any intimate matters. There was, on the contrary, a pressure to tolerate any situation in which derivatives of these early configurations were present in my patient's mind, and in mine, but could not be addressed in any direct or open way.

After a silence, the patient said she had telephoned her parents the previous evening to check that everything was all right and to confirm the arrangements for their arrival. She spoke to her father, who was preoccupied with the sleeping arrangements during their stay—in particular, with the possibility that he might have to share a double bed with her mother. The patient reassured him (reporting this in a slightly patronizing way) and said he should not worry, he would have a single bed to sleep in; she would sleep in the double. Father said, "What! have you got a *double bed*? What for? I didn't know you had a double bed!" My patient patiently explained that she had two singles in the main bedroom and a small double bed in the spare bedroom. She thought mother was probably kicking father by now, and he did not say any more. She was then silent for a long time. I thought it was clear that she was expecting me to take up the material that she had brought, and she had no intention of saying anything further about it herself.

I said I thought that she showed an anxiety similar to her father's about being too close to something, and she behaved as if it was important for her, too, to be in a single bed, apparently not really engaging with me or with the things she herself had spoken about. We knew that there was more that did go on, but it had to be kept hidden—in the loft, or locked up in cupboards.

She was then silent for a very long time. I found that this situation raised a number of difficulties. I thought the patient had brought material that related to her own images and fantasies of what went on between her parents, and also what she thought and felt about her father's manifest concern about *her* sleeping arrangements. I was familiar with the process whereby the patient reported some material to me and then seemed to withdraw to a single bed, as it were, leaving it up to me to address the material, which was often potentially exciting or disturbing for her. It never seemed to be useful for me to accept the responsibility for all the thinking and verbalizing in the session, and yet I felt I had to do something; I could not simply allow the session to pass in silence. I had thought carefully about my interpretation, and it had seemed a reasonable approach, and yet in the subsequent long silence it became clear to me that I was being treated exactly like her father—as someone who had behaved in an accusatory, intrusive fashion, which she could only deal with by withdrawal. I was thus felt as the oedipal father, much too preoccupied with his daughter's sexuality, and barely held back by mother's kick.

After a further long silence she said with an anxious note in her voice that she suddenly remembered that she had not put away her contraceptive pills. It would be o.k. unless people started looking in drawers. Maybe she could find a way, when her parents were there, to hide them quietly. After a short silence she said she was getting into a bit of a panic. It was then the end of the session, and she left in a slightly disorganized way, looking very anxious.

I think this material illustrates a number of features of importance to my patient. What appeared persistently was the view that the parental couple were involved in something violent and dangerous, an awful breaking through the hedge by a truck with a boiler on it which was out of control, and which the object barely survived. It was seen as not only difficult and dangerous for mother, but also something disturbing for father, and it was father's worries about the double bed that he communicated to her. This view of the parental intercourse helped to account for my patient's sexual anxieties, although what emerged, as her symptom diminished, was that the phantasy of a violent and destructive oedipal couple also contained a good deal of excitement for her and was often re-created in less threatening and more exciting forms, both inside and outside the analysis. The other aspect of the oedipal situation that emerged clearly here, and links with the first example, was the way in which the curiosity, jealousy and excitement may either be correctly perceived in the parental object, and/or projected into the parental object. Father's curiosity and preoccupation was more evident than his daughter's; indeed, his interest in my patient's activities was much more real than in the first patient I described.

This combination of perception and projection enabled the patient to avoid any contact with her own curiosity and jealousy, and this was evident both in the way she spoke of her parents and in her notable lack of interest in what happened in her analyst's life.

What interests me particularly is the way in which some of these issues became subtly enacted in the transference, so I was faced with the choice. I could have remained silent, avoiding becoming entangled with some of the powerful feelings of which she gave many indications, but this would not only have been unhelpful, it might also have expressed an anxious inhibition. When, on the other hand, I tried to take up the material in a way that I thought was appropriate, this led to my being made to feel that I had actually behaved in an inappropriate and intrusive way. One of the striking features of the transference situation in which I found myself was that I recognized that there was no way I could behave that was not imbued with the patient's intense projections and liable to evoke strong reactions in her. It was difficult to feel that there was anything I could do that would feel right.

The final point is that this situation was also re-lived over and over again in the patient's own mind. Not only did she behave in the analysis in an evasive, secretive and provocative way, hiding various exciting objects in the loft, but I think there was a more serious difficulty in her own thinking. Any connections that she made in her mind were liable to have the quality of a sudden and dangerous invasion—something that threatened the objects on which her life depended. Instead of making these links in her own mind, she used the analysis very skilfully to engender thoughts in me, to get me to make the connections, and she invited me to act in ways that she could defend herself against, because the threat was an external one. She feared that if her own thoughts became clearer and more direct, there would be no hedge to protect her, and there was a phantasy that the internal intercourse would be a catastrophic one. This need to maintain a variety of internal and external hedges led to a significant restriction in the quality of her thinking and in her capacity to be open or spontaneous, either in the analysis or in her social and sexual relationships.

I have a strong impression that these anxieties were based on experiences and phantasies that relate to her earliest object relationship—represented by the relation of mouth to nipple, which became imbued with fearful properties. She conveyed a picture of an anxious, rigid and obsessional mother whom it was very difficult to reach. I think this evoked in my patient a desperate, violent impulse to get through somehow. This impulse then became projected into the mother, whom she consequently perceived as threatening and intrusive. Her phantasy of the parental couple became, inevitably, invested with these qualities, with the penis coming to represent the violent intrusive nipple.

In the analysis, this patient used massive unconscious projective processes both to communicate and also to relieve herself of disturbance, but then she felt she had to protect herself from a violent and potentially destructive re-projection. In this patient, the parents are more clearly differentiated from one another than in the first case I referred to, and there is some belief in the possibility of a form of intercourse, although it is a very frightening and dangerous process. She *was* capable of clear thought and was often sharply perceptive, although, as I have indicated, she remained very frightened of the consequences of the coming together of her thoughts and phantasies when they related to primitive and intense feelings of love, excitement and destructiveness.

Discussion

I hope the clinical illustrations have given some indication of the nature of the oedipal phantasies prevalent in each of the patients at that time. Not only were the phantasies reflected in the patients' material, but one could follow the elements of the oedipal drama being re-enacted in the sessions. Through the operation of projective and introjective identification, the roles assigned, in phantasy, to patient and analyst were often complex and reversible. An example of this was the way the conflicts of the oedipal child became projected so it was the *analyst* who was confronted with the uncomfortable dilemmas.

One issue that these cases raise relates to the origin of the internal model of the parental couple (or the different versions of the couple, which co-exist). It will be partly based on the infant's accurate perceptions and intuitions regarding the nature of the couple of which he was a part in the early feeding situation, and later the oedipal couple with which he becomes preoccupied. Mrs. Klein has explored the ways in which the nature of the couple becomes distorted by the projection of qualities and phantasies into it for defensive or aggressive purposes. She also drew our attention to the importance of the envy that is aroused whenever the infant experiences his primary objects coming together to gratify one another. One of the ways of effecting the envious and jealous attacks is to project into the couple qualities that distort and spoil.

The infant is, of course, also the recipient of the projections of the parents, and the version of the oedipal couple that becomes established in him may be partly the result of the projection of the model of the couple that exists in the mind of the couple itself. In the third case, for example, I believe the patient's mother had a view of any intimate contact—whether feeding or sexual intercourse— as being intrusive and disturbing, and this was projected into my patient. In the material relating to the double bed, her father also communicated his discomfort and reluctance to be too intimately involved with mother.

In the analysis, the relative importance of these different factors in the evolution of the internal model of the oedipal couple will always be difficult to assess and will often alter as one's understanding of the patient changes.

In this chapter I have also tried to indicate that the phantasy of the oedipal couple is closely related to the way in which the patient is able to use his mind to create links between his thoughts and feelings, and to tolerate the anxieties that result from such links. If the anxieties associated with the phantasy of the parental couple are too great, then there will be a corresponding interference with the capacity for making connections between elements in the patient's mind, a process that seems to depend, in some essential way, on the phantasy associated with the conjunction of mouth and nipple, or penis and vagina.

Bion has made an important contribution to our understanding of the pathology of the patient's experience of any couple (Bion, 1959). He refers to the patient's disposition to attack the link between two objects, the prototype of which is the link between the mouth and the breast, which arouses the infant's hatred and envy. He suggests that even when the infant is a participant in a creative act, sharing an enviable emotional experience, he is also identified with the excluded party, with the consequent pain, envy and jealousy. (Thus, following Mrs. Klein, he postulates a very early form of Oedipus complex.) The response of the infant to the experience, or phantasy of the creative link—first between mouth and breast, later between the sexual parents—is attacked and transformed into a hostile and destructive sexuality, rendering the couple sterile. This may take the form of an attack on the mother's or the parents' state of mind, or an understanding that may develop between patient and analyst.

The understanding of the way the infant's envy becomes aroused by the parental couple, with a violent and disruptive projection into the couple in order to separate them or make them sterile, has illuminated many of the pathological versions of the oedipal situation with which we are confronted in our patients.

The other process I have referred to also results in the patient's experience of the oedipal couple as being engaged in some bizarre and often violent interaction, but it seems to have a different origin and is based on a different mechanism. In this case the infant is not confronted with a creative couple, arousing his envy, but a parental figure or a couple that he finds impenetrable, unable properly to receive or respond to his projections. This may give rise to violent attempts to get through, with the paranoid anxieties that were most clear in my third patient, or to a sense of a hopeless and bizarre situation that cannot be faced, as with the first patient.

These alternatives raise interesting and difficult diagnostic problems, as each may require a different approach. I have the impression that in each of the three cases, although the history and pathology were different, there was a phantasy of a very disordered oedipal couple— in the first case, for example, a couple who could not really come together properly, and in the third case, a situation where one is faced either with not being able to penetrate the hedge at all or having to do so with such violence that it might be catastrophic.

I have tried to illustrate how these configurations are vividly brought into the transference, presenting the analyst with some of the dilemmas with which the patient is constantly faced. I have also tried to show the link between the way in which the oedipal situation is construed internally and the patient's capacity to think, as any real understanding is dependent on the identification with a couple capable of a creative intercourse.

REFERENCES

Bion, W. R. (1959). Attacks on linking. *Int. J. Psycho-Anal., 40,* 308–315. [Reprinted in *Second Thoughts* (pp. 93–109). London: Heinemann, 1967.]

Klein, M. (1928). Early stages of the Oedipus conflict. *Int. J. Psycho-Anal., 9,* 167–180. [Reprinted in *The Writings of Melanie Klein, 1* (pp. 186–198). London: Hogarth Press, 1975.]

———— (1932). *The Psychoanalysis of Children*. [Reprinted in *The Writings of Melanie Klein, 2*. London: Hogarth Press, 1975.]

Steiner, J. (1985). Turning a blind eye: the cover-up for Oedipus. *Int. Rev. Psychoanal., 12*, 161–172.

CHAPTER FOUR

The invisible Oedipus complex

Edna O'Shaughnessy

A current controversy about the Oedipus complex is whether it is indeed universal and of central importance, still to be regarded as 'the nuclear complex of development'. It is a clinical fact that there are long periods of analysis—possibly, some have suggested, even whole analyses—in which there seem to be little or even no oedipal material. In trying to account for this fact, analysts have taken different ways. One way, taken by Kohut and his followers (Kohut, 1971), is to set the Oedipus complex aside, posit a theory of self-psychology and advise a new clinical technique, which focuses on deficit and offers restoration. Kleinians take an opposite way. Their approach, when the Oedipus complex is what I am calling 'invisible', is that this is so, not because it is unimportant, but because it is so important and felt by the patient (from whatever causes) to be so unnegotiable that he employs psychic means to make and keep it invisible.

In this chapter I focus on one small area of the Oedipus

complex: its first stages, when these are reached after a disturbed early development. When Klein (1928, 1932) added early stages and later linked the Depressive Position, on which in her view mental health depends, to Freud's nuclear complex, she expanded the emotional constellation from which the Oedipus complex of each patient takes its very individual form. The patients I describe are struggling to obliterate an early oedipal situation, which feels continually to be threatening. As will become apparent, feelings of exclusion, problems of separateness and of being single in the presence of an oedipal pair, and, above all, a distinctive type of sexual splitting are foremost in these patients.

I begin with a detailed account of Leon, who at 11 years of age is nearing puberty, but whose mental life is still largely occupied by defences against his disturbed relations to his primary objects and a traumatic early oedipal constellation. His presenting problem was panic at any new prospect. A move to secondary school was looming when he began his analysis, and his parents thought he would never manage it. Otherwise, they told me—though father seemed not quite convinced—there were 'no problems'. He was 'just an ordinary boy'. Leon was their first child, followed closely by a second, another boy, conceived when Leon was four months old. Leon's younger brother was a head taller, rowdy and active, while Leon stayed in his room with a book, although he would go out to play if a friend took the initiative. Only with difficulty could his mother bring herself to talk about Leon's infancy, which she said was 'terrible'. He had cried for hours; she could not bear that, or the feeding. 'Not what I expected,' she kept repeating. This limited and, particularly on the mother's side, uninsightful picture of Leon—intolerable as an infant, and now, his anxieties unrecognized, with parents not expecting him to want or to be able to manage life—foretold accurately part of what unfolded in the analysis.

On the first day Leon placed himself near and opposite me, seating himself with a sort of screwing-in movement on a little bench in-between two cushions. Except for two sessions, during the first 18 months of analysis he left his bench only to go to the toilet. He watched me through two different pairs of glasses—one like his mother's, the other like his father's—checking the room or myself for the smallest movement or change. Any change made him acutely anxious. He seemed younger than his years, a depressed, lumpy, soft boy, who conveyed that he had almost no hope of being understood. His appearance could change astonishingly. He could 'become' and look like some version of his father, or 'become' and look like his mother; he also 'became' a small sick infant, and at times he looked strangely enlarged. These changing appearances were due, I think, to his projection into and almost total identification with his objects on an early feeling level. The figures he let into—or which he felt forced themselves into—his inner world, he experienced in a similarly physical and concrete way; they possessed him, and he personified them. Leon experienced analysis as a disturbance that he was both against and also for, sometimes gratefully so. He said once, 'I don't want you, I need you.'

In the beginning, after inserting himself between his cushions and checking the room quickly for change, he spent his sessions staring silently at the floor below or the door opposite him. I elicited that he saw dots on the floor, that they 'pulled him in' and 'made him dizzy', but that by looking away he could get out. About the door he said he 'saw patterns'. He pointed out what he called a 'pattern': distinctly a penis with testicles. He described how the door moved nearer and nearer, but if he left the room and came back, the door would be at its proper distance again. He reported these events in a matter-of-fact voice in answer to questions over many sessions, the anxiety that underlay these near hallucinations and his fascination with them totally split off. He seemed to be fragmenting into dots and patterns two terrifying internal objects and emptying them out of his mind onto the floor and the door. There he watched them, withdrawn from contact with myself or the playroom, trying to stay in control and to remain free of anxiety and emotional content. He could never succeed in staying mentally void and withdrawn for long. Momentarily, terror pushed into him, or a flash of hatred of me, or acute depression, or a sudden tenderness. He would quickly rid himself of these intense contradictory feelings, which pushed and pulled him about. He had an ongoing conflict whether to withdraw or whether to allow contact, a conflict indicated by his feet, which retreated under his bench, came out towards me and then retreated again. Sometimes he blocked his ears, more often he listened intently. After the first few months his enormous latent anxiety was greatly lessened, which brought him much relief. And, to his parents' astonishment, he managed the move to secondary school without panic.

This brings me now to the subject of Leon's Oedipus complex. It was possible and necessary to continue to interpret his fear of the smallest change, his need of an empty mind, his wish to keep me always curious and closely attentive, his chronic anxiety that I would not understand him, but come too close, or force his feelings back into him, etc., etc. But between whom and what were these processes occurring? What was the symbolic significance or equivalence of Leon's inserting himself between two cushions on the bench? What was the meaning of the movement and change he dreaded? What or who was I in the transference? In Leon's denuded universe I found it difficult to speak of meaning: it sounded artificial, and if I persisted it also aroused his anxiety and hatred.

To consider this more closely, if I interpreted that he did not expect me to understand him, he sometimes acknowledged such an interpretation with relief and, I came to

notice, with more than a hint of a gloat. However, if I went a
step further and spoke of myself as being like an inadequate
parent, he became anxious. 'No! You're not like my Mum.'
One issue that emerged was that he heard me as being
disparaging of his mother and father and narcissistically
implying that I was superior to them. This aroused his
loyalty to his parents and, in addition, a fear of forming a
nasty collusion with me against them. Beyond this,
however, there was something more important. If I referred
to myself as a parent in the transference, Leon became
enraged and anxious; in contrast, if I interpreted his
projection into me of a confused watching child while he felt
he was being a cruelly indifferent father or mother (often, I
thought, one of the dynamics in his sessions), Leon liked
especially that bit of the interpretation in which I referred
to myself as the child. He received it with satisfaction, as if
to say, 'Ah, you admit it. You *are* a child.' Thus, while
seeming to comply with the view that he had parents who
had supposedly arranged for him to have something called
psychoanalysis, a part of him privately held another view of
the proceedings: he was big, his parents and I were little,
and he had attractive superior activities—the dizzy pull of
the floor and the nearing of the door—and from on high he
watched our little goings on, sometimes even protecting us.
In one of his rare spontaneous remarks he said to me loftily,
'I know all your little habits. I know the way your watch on
your arm slips around. I know the way your shoe slips off.'
These two selected observations are accurate. I thought
their meaning was that he knew how my watch—that is, his
mother's eye—had the habit of slipping round him and not
really seeing him. And he also knew his father's habit of not
staying in himself and slipping off, i.e. projecting himself
into and getting too close and involved with Leon. But Leon
did not want these 'little habits' to be transference
phenomena with a dimension of meaning such as my watch
to be linked to an eye. He cut the links between his inner

world and his analysis, which he stripped of meaning, and he wanted me to accept and to adopt his disconnections and also to endorse his omnipotent phantasy of reversal—that he was big and I was little—and to join him in this as in other things.

I was also at this period drawing Leon's attention to how he mostly spoke softly, to draw me near to him to hear, and also how I had to come to him with questions, as he rarely spoke voluntarily. I interpreted that he felt that he pulled me so near that I became like the cushions next to him. I pointed out that he wanted me to stay very close, never disturb him, not make any connections or expect him to change, while he sat and looked on from on high, unmoving. Leon agreed that this was what he wanted. He also amplified with further freely given accounts of himself when I related what he let me see in the playroom to his daydreaming at school and his liking to stay in his room at home. But when I tried to explore the meaning (almost always there seemed to be some part of his ego for which meaning remained a possibility in spite of his continual stripping) of his high observatory, interpreting, however gradually, that with the movements he made when he sat down he imagined that he inserted himself into a home in mother's body, there to be the baby inside, or that he felt he held mother and father down on either side of him and so prevented their moving and coming together, or that sometimes he felt altered and big and saw me from afar as small, Leon was both enraged and disturbed. Often he rushed out of the room to the toilet, blocked his ears on return and told me, 'I hate your talking.'

At such moments, instead of being his cushions—he once explained he did not mind other little changes in the room, so long as the cushions did not move—he saw me exercising my analytic function. I then became parents who move and so destroy his phantasy of being inside. His rush out of the room expressed his momentary ejection from his seat on the bench, a change that made him hate me.

It is interesting to return for a moment to the beginning of his analysis, to the time when a change first occurred. By checking the room and knowing the fixed routine of his sessions, Leon was maintaining an overall phantasy world of no change, no separateness, and no separations—the gap between sessions or at weekends did not exist for him. This routine was first altered by my not working on a Monday Bank holiday. He failed to arrive for the last session of the preceding week; during his hour his father telephoned in a panic, saying he had arranged to meet his wife and son at the Underground and then bring Leon to me, but they were not there.

On the Tuesday Leon arrived, wearing no spectacles. At first he was terrified of being punished and pushed out of his home on his bench or even out of analysis altogether for missing a session, and he was relieved when I interpreted his acute anxiety. Then he tried to re-establish me as his cushion close to him, staying silent, making little movements to get me attentive and around him. After this he told me he had dropped his glasses during the weekend, and they had smashed. He then stared short-sightedly at the door on which he said there were 'waves', and the floor, on which he said there were 'bits not as nice'. I think Leon had found the changed routine unbearable, could not come, had smashed his sight and smashed also the objects of which 'waves' and 'not nice bits' were the residues, but so residual that it was impossible to know what he had fragmented and expelled.

After eight months or so of analysis, Leon was more able to bear contact with the content of his psychic life, and then the nature of the change he dreaded became clear as over widely spaced sessions bits of his early oedipal situation returned. First there was his move from the bench, to sit for the first time at the table. He took out a pack of cards, and we played a game. He was secretly enormously pleased to have moved. The next day he again sat at the table. He took out a different pack of cards. During the game he said, 'These cards are someone else's. They are nicer than mine,' speaking as if stating a fact accepted by him and me. He never brought cards again, and for ten months more never moved from his bench. Through this painful episode he gave me a glimpse of the trauma that the birth of his brother had been and still is to him, and of his belief in a family presumption that his brother was nicer than he. Leon showed me that he surrendered and did not compete; for a long while he never tried again in the playroom, just as he did not try at home or at school.

Following the two sessions with the cards, he resorted to various manoeuvres to find out the next holiday dates without actually *asking*. When I told him the dates, he gave one of his rare smiles and said 'O.K.', nodding his head happily. Then, with the approach of the break, several early oedipal feelings pressed into consciousness.

On the last day of the week Leon brought a roll of sweets. He asked me if I would *like one,* slightly emphasizing 'like' and 'one'. I interpreted that he wished to know whether I liked what he was offering and, really, whether I liked him. I went on to say that he was expressing his longing for me as a mother who had only him, rather than the mother who had his brother, too. Leon was furious. He pushed and pulled the knobs on his electronic wrist watch very fast, saying angrily, 'I'm getting the time right.' I said he felt I had mentioned his brother at the wrong time, just when he was longing to have me to himself, and rage and disappointment were now pushing and pulling him about. I linked these feelings to his infancy, and how the baby that was still there in him felt that his mother, by becoming pregnant when he was four months old, filled herself with his brother at the wrong time, because he still needed to have her for himself. Leon continued to push and pull furiously at his watch, all his sweetness gone. He rushed out to the toilet, returned looking empty, and became very sleepy. However, when he said good-bye, he nodded his head, as if to say 'O.K.'

On the Monday he was burdened, and instead of cursorily checking that the room was the same he kept looking curiously about. He spoke longingly of 'the chair with the cushion' at the far end of the room. This 'chair with the cushion' was more capacious, and he would be more comfortable, and as it is not opposite me he would not be closely watched or watching me. He said with great pain that it was 'far'. I am not certain what this 'chair with a cushion' meant to him, but it was the first time Leon had seen a place he wanted to get to and realized he could not, that it was at the moment too far for him. With insight into himself it was a widening of horizons.

He did not look at the 'far' chair in the next few sessions. He restricted the area on which he used his eyes to the small patch of the floor beneath him. Each time he was about to speak, he put his hand over his mouth and stopped himself. He became withdrawn and then despondent. When I spoke to him about the strong force in him that stopped him talking and moving, and how he felt hopeless about ever being able to reach what he longed for, he was very moved.

The last session of the week was again different. Leon came in without looking at me—not even when I opened the front door to him—and in the playroom he kept me entirely out of his vision. I interpreted that he did not want to see me because at the end of the week I was his going-away analyst. As if a shock-wave were passing through him, Leon's whole body shook. Then he kicked violently in my direction and made a rude gesture of 'up you'. He split off his feelings and became aloof. He said coldly, 'I am looking forward to the holidays.' I agreed that he was, that he wanted to be free of me, now a hateful disturbance to him. 'Yes,' he answered with a cruel smile. I remarked on his cruel satisfaction, and he was instantly anxious, rushing out to the toilet; when he returned, he listened intently to my voice to assess my state of mind. When I next looked at him, I had a shock. Quite unconsciously he had bulged his jacket out like a pregnant woman, and his face had changed and become his mother's. He sat looking more and more suffering and unloved. I think he had incorporated and was totally identified with an analyst/mother whom he had cruelly called 'a hateful disturbance'. When I said that he seemed to be feeling the suffering inside of him of his unloved pregnant mother, Leon's face worked in distress. For a moment it was real grief. Then he looked angry and anxious. Somewhere in the house a noise sounded. The word 'man' was drawn unwillingly from him: 'M–A–N,' he said. It was his recognition of father's presence when mother was pregnant with his brother.

When the session ended, he was both trying desperately to pull me closely round him by his usual methods, and also repeatedly making three taps in a very menacing way, indicating how again and again there is a hateful, threatening three. As he was going, he prodded the wall as if feeling its solidarity and sensing the barring quality of a baby or perhaps a father who closes mother to him.

The end of this sequence was on the Monday. Leon looked different, for the first time like a boy nearing puberty, in smart trousers, such as a twelve-year-old might choose. At first he was more communicative and active than usual, but as the session went on he was in increasing conflict—his feet coming out and going back under his bench—whether to continue to go forward or retreat.

In the last week he became a high onlooker from his position between the cushions. The sessions were immobilized, and there were no significant elements, dyadic or oedipal. The coming holiday was idealized. He said he was glad to get away because here it was 'empty' and 'boring'.

His Oedipus complex was not the kind where sexual desire for mother and sexual rivalry with father are foremost. Leon started not with a parental pair, but with a menacing three—mother pregnant with a new baby and father. There was no rivalry; instead, as he showed in the sessions with the playing cards, there was surrender. Leon competed neither with his sibling nor with his father—he retreated. The onset of the oedipal situation was so intolerable to him that he expelled his own and his parents' sexuality. When he started analysis, his internal sexual objects were ejected onto the floor and the door, and he looked sexless. On the floor was a confused vagina and mouth, minutely fragmented into dots that sucked him in or made him dizzy, which he saw as 'not as nice'. On the door was a more intact father's penis, alarmingly invasive, reduced to a pattern, which was what it was for Leon—his predominant identification was with his father.

In the earliest stages of the Oedipus complex the infant has phantasies of mother containing father's penis or the whole father, and of father combining with mother's breasts and vagina, all in a state of perpetual gratification. Leon's feelings of exclusion and frustration would have been enormously increased by a new baby in reality inside mother enjoying all that he phantasized was granted in mother's interior.

Foremost for Leon was the problem of separateness. At four months, his mother's pregnancy came at the wrong time in his development, when he still needed an exclusive relationship for the reception of his projections—all the more because of his disastrous start. He was still in the paranoid–schizoid position, on the brink of the depressive position, old relations to part-objects overlapping with emerging relations to whole objects. The perception of a 'going-away' analyst sent a shock-wave through him. He felt ejected and instantly made a two-pronged attacking entry of 'up you' on the pregnant mother. The sweetness there was in him on the 1:1 basis he longed for with his mother was gone, and his hatred turned cruel. Pregnant, she was unloved by him, and when Leon sensed her suffering, he felt a grief more than he could bear making him angry and anxious. His ego could not cope: it was pushed and pulled about by a succession of unmanageable emotions. At the first cancelled session near the start of his analysis he even had to smash his glasses and stay away. Now that his ego was a little stronger, he could allow elements of his Oedipus complex to return, to see mother, new baby and father, which affected his own identity. Instead of sexlessness and seeing the world through mother's and father's glasses because of being in a state of projective identification with one or other of them, he had a proper boyishness about him for the first time, even though he did not maintain it for long. He was soon again in conflict whether to go forward or retreat. As the break drew near, he dispersed his oedipal experiences, which were invisible as he inserted himself in omnipotent phantasy into and between objects with whom he stayed and which were his cushions.

Leon's cushions are de-sexualized parents whom he holds apart and around himself—the comfortable remainders from which frightening components have been expelled onto the floor and the door. Because these expelled objects are so minutely fragmented or denuded into a mere pattern, the nature of the sexual splitting that has taken place is difficult to see. In other patients like Leon for whom the earliest stages of the Oedipus complex constitute a fixation point this is more possible. Melanie Klein writes, 'this (the combined parent figure) is one of the phantasy formations characteristic of the earliest stages of the Oedipus complex and which, if maintained in strength is detrimental both to object relations and sexual development' (Klein, 1952, p. 55).

In my view, a most important feature of this constellation is that the projective identification that aims to separate and attack the sexual parents *fractures a combination.* Because the emotional level is early, the objects of the fracture are in any case already distorted by unretrieved projections, but through their fracture and further projections their heterosexual procreative qualities are destroyed, and the patient has instead pathological sexual objects—distorted, incomplete and broken open. Often the father is seen not as father or husband but as a sadistic, phallic male, and the mother becomes a weak, open masochistic female, both felt to be open to homosexual alliances against the other sex. These phantasies are so omnipotent that the patient believes he has achieved a separation of the sexes and will, for instance, have dreams about and make references to women, but always with women or girls, and men are again always with other men or with boys.

For instance, one of my patients saw the analyst who fetched him from the waiting room as female, over-sensitive and too eager to be empathic and nice to him. Once he was on the couch, he felt I had changed. I was male, high, aloof and condescending, and he immediately projected himself into this figure, becoming totally like it.

A patient I analysed many years ago brought his fractured images in a dream.

He was in a foreign country. There were two houses apart from each other, each with a tennis court. In one house, though there was no sign of it on the outside, he knew there was a woman inside with a corset and stockings wanting to have sex; the surface of the tennis court of this house was cracked. The surface of the tennis court of the other house was intact. There, two men were facing each other, playing very competitive tennis without a net.

This patient has split apart the early oedipal couple and maintained separate relations to each. His dream illustrates how profoundly affected both his sexual life and his object relations were. For him, the mother was an evidently cracked and seductive female, wanting sex from him—one-half of his predominant perception of me in the transference for a long time. At the start of analysis he was himself highly erotized, feeling almost totally identified with a mad, promiscuous female—promiscuous sex with promiscuous women was one of his problems. During adolescence this patient had felt he was in a feminine body with breasts, a transexual feeling so near to delusion that he had been unable to undress in the changing rooms at school or swim without a vest to conceal his chest. The seductive woman in the house in his dream was thus also himself inside his mother. Apart, meanwhile, males played a watchful, competitive face-to-face game, with no way of knowing the true score. This was the other half of his transference, which corresponded to the area of his life, his career, which on the surface was intact, although he was enormously envious and competitive with me (as he was with his business associates) and believed me to be so with him, both of us cheating to win. Often, in these cases, the analyst is made into a watcher, while the patient repeatedly acts out sexually with unsuitable partners in painful triangles, where possession of one excludes and makes hostile another of the combination.

Leon fractured the combined parent in a rather similar way to the patient who split me between waiting and consulting room. As we were able to see later in the analysis, as mother I was to be drawn away from father, come closer around him and coax him with questions, not only when he was anxious and needed me to, but also when he was hostile and chose not to relate to me. His feeling then was that I was no more a mother but a little girl, too soft, who does not confront his hostility but cushions it, with abasement and pleading that turns into a horrific masochistic sucking him in. The cushion on his other side was a caricature of father, stupidly idealizing the practical and ordinary, cruelly aloof from meaning and marriage, and wanting instead to come too close and pair with Leon.

With respect to the early Oedipus complex following on faulty early development, there are two aspects that drive the patient to fracture and obliterate out of sight the combined oedipal parents. The first of these is the stimulation of this primitive primal scene. Leon, for instance, felt pushed and pulled about by an onslaught of feelings beyond the limited capacity of his ego to tolerate. The second aspect arises from the fundamental fact that the primal scene excludes the patient. At this early stage, and especially when there has been an excessive use of projective identification to compensate for disturbed object relations, exclusion is experienced as ejection from the object. The patient feels not only impossibly stimulated but also outside and alone—twin aspects I hope to illustrate with some brief material from Mr. A.

Mr. A, an intelligent and sensitive man, was married and a father. Earlier in his life he had had several homosexual relationships, and under pressure he still had strong homosexual inclinations. Among his reasons for coming to me for an analysis was tormenting jealousy of his wife. He thought she was betraying him sexually—but he was not sure whether she really was or whether he was only tormenting himself with phantasies. If he saw her speak on the telephone or make herself ready to go out, he saw her planning, and almost having, sex with someone else.

There were many strands in Mr. A's analysis that I must ignore to focus on what is relevant to this chapter. In some respects Mr. A was like Leon. He was affectionate, and he had a strong death instinct and at depth a conviction of fundamental non-acceptance by a narcissistic and otherwise preoccupied mother. Mr. A lacked a securely internalized good object and used projective identification and omnipotent control as his main methods of operating with his objects. Unlike Leon, an early pregnancy played no part in shaping his Oedipus complex, for Mr. A was the youngest sibling. The adverse external circumstance in his family was the degree of overt sexual disturbance. Father and mother seemed to have had some homosexual inclinations, and from the age of 13 an elder brother had had sexual relations with my patient. Since debased sexual figures were both the result of Mr. A's projections and fracture of the oedipal pair, and also really corresponded to his actual parents to some extent (and later to other real objects), Mr. A was often confused and suffered a loss of reality sense; he became terrified there were no objects with whom reality testing was possible.

Unlike Leon, Mr. A was psychically highly mobile, and during the analysis he was highly erotized. He aimed for instant penetration and possession to take him away from confusion and anxiety. The need to feel inside his object, not to be out and single, to be instantly recognized and form an excited pair was paramount in Mr. A and was (in addition to identifications) the driving force behind his homosexuality. In the beginning he stripped the relation between patient and analyst of transference meaning—it was he and I, personal. I was an idealized 'new' object who would give him what he had failed to find before, and give it to him in a way he could tolerate, with no exclusion, no waiting, without stimulating anxiety or guilt or envy or jealousy or wounding his narcissism. Mostly he was excited by homosexual phantasy in which he was inside a high phallus looking down on and in control of me—a boy who would admire and serve him. But if I disturbed him in some way, he turned cold and cruel. Sometimes he was in a state of projective identification with an effeminate, softer, more corrupt figure. The sexes were always split. This erotized homosexual transference and a conviction of perverse erotized relations obtaining everywhere was for a long time an enclave disconnected from his oedipal situation. Oedipal figures were nowhere in view, in or out of analysis, and nor was the child in Mr. A.

As his excitement lessened, he grew watchful. He started to see 'signs' in the room, or my clothes, speech, of intimacies, parties, sex, etc., which invited him or excluded him—he could not tell which. Confused oedipal delusions and doubts about my sexuality were hidden in his material. Had I been, was I perhaps still, actually excited and over-involved with him, as he was with me? It was so painful a period of his analysis that I would say Mr. A was in anguish as his deep oedipal suspicions, delusions and confusions emerged. His paranoid feelings decreased gradually, and he allowed me more contact with his shame, disappointment, anxiety and depression about his objects and himself.

As his sexual delusions faded in the transference, he began sometimes to feel painfully exposed to an oedipal pair who do not consummate his phantasies but exclude him. There were very considerable difficulties in his life at this time, and Mr. A was more easily disturbed by 'signs' than was usual at this stage. An important detail is that on the day of the session I report I was more formally dressed than usual.

The instant he saw me when I fetched him from the waiting room he looked anxious and dark in the face. On the couch he was silent for a long time. Then he said he had had a dream, and speaking fast and sounding both desperate and excited he said he was in France, and he had gone to a restaurant, and he had ordered 'tête de veau', and when the waiter brought it, it was on the plate without its eyes, black eye sockets, vacant mouth, black stuff, mushrooms, neck standing up. ... He went on and on. He paused, waiting, I thought, for me to interpret something about a chopped-off head or unseeing eyes. However, the effect of his rapid relating of what he was calling a dream—which I think was really a swift flight into psychotic phantasy—had been to project chaos and disturbance into me. Mr. A continued: 'Then there was some string—do you say "fiselle?" This is what I ordered. Or was it "cervelle"?. ...' He paused again.

After a while he spoke about a frill on a chamber pot, or a cake oozing out over the edge, and so on. When he stopped, I interpreted that he had gone into the world of his dream and wished me to join him there, to get away from the chaos and disturbance that the sight of my suit had caused in him. He answered, 'I had my eye shut. I was thinking of analysis, anal Isis. Suit? What suit? Oh, you mean your *suit*. ...' Mr. A continued mocking me and falsely pretending not to know what I was talking about. I suggested that when he saw me and now when I spoke to him, he felt controlled, ordered to notice my suit and talk about it, on top of being made to feel so disturbed and chaotic by it, and that this was so offensive to him that it drove him to mockery and pretense.

At slower speed Mr. A continued with his French 'dream' or theme with more variations, but his excitement was lessening. He ended saying in a bitter voice, 'Proust's Charlus ordered some rough trade and all he saw was his parents "doing it"'. I said I thought he was describing his experiences in the session. The rough trade he wanted was having me join him in his world of homosexual phantasy, but what he became aware of instead was me at my job, that is, parents 'doing it', which made him feel bitter and sneering. After a long silence Mr. A said, 'But why?' He paused, and said 'We are not there together. I'm alone.' He began to cry, saying, 'It's ridiculous to feel like this.'

Melanie Klein writes, 'Sometimes the analyst appears simultaneously to represent both parents—in that case often in a hostile alliance against the patient, whereby the negative transference acquires great intensity' (Klein, 1952, pp. 54–55). My suit is the 'sign' of a hostile primal pair, who are so enormously disturbing to Mr. A that he is impelled to perverse defensive and destructive phantasies. Previously, Mr. A would have immersed himself in homosexual phantasies for sessions; he would have become increasingly aloof and persecuted and ended with a masochistic depression. In this session, he and I could get through his fast, massive defences against oedipal disturbance and stimulation, and he recovered his contact with me and himself. He was then aware of his parents' 'doing it', his hostility to their intercourse and his bitter feelings of betrayal. The boy in the man was suddenly on the couch, and he felt alone and cast out, and he cried.

Before I conclude, a brief word on technique. Mr. A pressured the analyst to join him in rough homosexual trade, as Leon pressured the analyst to be a cushion in unchangingness and meaninglessness. Part of the pressure to 'act in' with the patient is the pressure to formulate interpretations that accept that rough trade or unchangingness and meaninglessness are all there is. The patient invites the analyst to ignore the mental work he has done, and which he is still doing in the session, to keep invisible an early oedipal situation he is endeavouring to control and obliterate.

To give one small example from Leon's material: when he brought sweets and asked if I would *like one,* simply to interpret his longing to be my only one in this session would not take into account the full situation—viz., that he was trying to make invisible and induce me, too, to annihilate the fact of a weekend break which meant that I as mother shut him out because I had another baby. The fuller interpretation of his longing for a mother who was not also the mother of his brother enabled him to express rather than keep split-off his rage at a mother forcing a brother on him at the wrong time. With Mr. A, there was the opposite problem in the session reported. His pressure was not, as with Leon, to go too slowly or not go at all, but to go too fast, to rush to interpret the content of his dream. Had I done so, I think he would have felt that he had fractured the combined parents and annexed me to himself homosexually in 'rough trade'. As it was, he felt the parents stayed firm, and were 'doing it'—i.e. that I had stayed at my job of understanding the emotional chaos and disturbance the oedipal combination caused him.

Naturally, an analyst has to try to sense afresh in every session what is urgent and near enough to be potentially dynamic. In other sessions, the exploration of Leon's primal need for a 1:1 relationship, or the meaning of the details of Mr. A's swift phantasies, may be where the emotional dynamic is.

Summary

Leon and Mr. A belong to a group of patients whose Oedipus complex is not part of a normal developmental thrust with sexual desire and jealous rivalry foremost. Awareness of an oedipal pair, because of their ongoing defenses against their continuing early impairment, is forced upon them. It is almost intolerable, and they use further defenses to make and keep it invisible. I thus disagree with the Kohutian view of deficit with no Oedipus complex in these cases.

Above all, because projective identification into the object has become their mode of coping with their disturbed relations to their original object, awareness of a combined figure ejects them from their projective home inside the object. In addition, the combined parents—a cruel structure in these cases—demand sexual watching, threaten invasion or suction into their perpetual intercourse, stimulate envy, and enormously increase anxiety and depression. Because the patient lacks an internalized figure that can contain and modify this nearly overwhelming state of mind, he feels alone with an intolerable psychic load and threatening chaos. To disburden his psyche and re-enter his object, the patient in phantasy inserts himself between the combined figure, pulls the couple apart, and projects himself into one or other of the separated pair. These exclusive relations, however, differ significantly from earlier pre-oedipal ones. His objects, distorted already by unretrieved projections, now bear the marks of the defensive and attacking fracture of their sexual combination, so that the patient feels himself to be in a world not of oedipal figures but of debased and damaged sexual objects. This form of splitting an object in the early stages of the Oedipus complex is so distinctive in its effect that it should, I think, be known by the special name of fracturing an object. Leon's sexless immobilization and Mr. A's homosexuality, both with at times near-delusional confusion, are two of the many forms this constellation takes; pathological sexual relations in a triangular framework are also characteristic.

Finally, because of their lack of an internal good object, these patients feel little capable of bearing singleness. They must be in a state of projective identification with another object. In Leon's analysis singleness is not yet even a dynamic, and Mr. A, well on in his analysis, is still in distress when he perceives the parental couple and feels alone. For them the oedipal story begins there—cast out. This, after all, is where the original myth began: Laius cast out Oedipus.

REFERENCES

Klein, M. (1928). Early stages of the Oedipus conflict. *Int. J. Psycho-Anal.*, *9*, 167–180. [Reprinted in *The Writings of Melanie Klein, 1* (pp. 186–198). London: Hogarth Press, 1975.]

———— (1932). *The Psychoanalysis of Children.* [Reprinted in *The Writings of Melanie Klein, 2.* London: Hogarth Press, 1975.]

———— (1952). The origins of transference. *Int. J. Psycho-Anal.*, *33*, 433–438. [Reprinted in *The Writings of Melanie Klein, 3* (pp. 48–56). London: Hogarth Press, 1975.]

Kohut H. (1971). *The Analysis of the Self.* New York: International Universities Press.

INDEX